Reporting

Reporting Conflict

James Rodgers

palgrave
macmillan

First published 2012 by
PALGRAVE MACMILLAN

Palgrave Macmillan in the UK is an imprint of Macmillan Publishers Limited, registered in England, company number 785998, of Houndmills, Basingstoke, Hampshire RG21 6XS.

Palgrave Macmillan in the US is a division of St Martin's Press LLC, 175 Fifth Avenue, New York, NY 10010.

Palgrave Macmillan is the global academic imprint of the above companies and has companies and representatives throughout the world.

Palgrave® and Macmillan® are registered trademarks in the United States, the United Kingdom, Europe and other countries.

ISBN-13: 978–0–230–27446–4

This book is printed on paper suitable for recycling and made from fully managed and sustained forest sources. Logging, pulping and manufacturing processes are expected to conform to the environmental regulations of the country of origin.

A catalogue record for this book is available from the British Library.

A catalog record for this book is available from the Library of Congress.

10 9 8 7 6 5 4 3 2 1
21 20 19 18 17 16 15 14 13 12

Printed and bound in Great Britain by
CPI Antony Rowe, Chippenham and Eastbourne

To Mette, for understanding why I wanted to go to those places

of rumour, those moments of insight, twists of confusion, trepidation and hope. Later that night my mobile phone lit up in the dark. 'Allan,' the voice says, 'you should see what is going on here. It is Vietnam in the desert.'

The voice belonged to an old friend, a journalist I have known over more than ten years in other people's wars. He has crossed the Euphrates north of Nasariyah with the United States Marine Corps and what he is seeing fills him with foreboding. He cannot move more than a few dozen metres from the Lieutenant Colonel's tent. From this narrow perspective he is coming to this view.

'The Americans are moving through the country in terror of what lies beyond every horizon', he says. 'Every civilian is a potential suicide bomber to them. They see every town and village as a menace, a harbour for terrorism.'

By now, US troops were at the gates of Baghdad. As we waited for the end I thought of those I had once known in Baghdad, when I was there during the First Gulf War in 1991, and I wondered whether I would ever see them again. I thought of my man from the ministry. My Iraqi minder. The man whose job it was to serve the monstrous regime, to be the conduit for its propaganda, the man who had had to look me in the eye and tell me as sincerely as he could that Kuwait was the nineteenth province of Iraq, and that the glorious and beloved leader Saddam Hussein would prevail by turning the sands of Arabia red with the blood of US servicemen. He didn't mean it. It was obvious.

One night in the war of 1991 we sat in the darkness of the blacked-out city waiting for the missiles. We were in the garden of the Al Rasheed Hotel and I had just sent the last of that day's reports back to London by satellite phone. We were utterly alone. 'Tell me honestly,' I said. 'Do you believe that stuff? Do you believe any of it?'

'Listen to me,' he said. He was daring to be candid. It took courage, real courage. 'I have an eight-year-old son, and two daughters who are a little older than him. We are very proud of them. But since this war began my brave little boy can scarcely go the toilet by himself, he is so afraid of everything. Should we have pulled out of Kuwait before all this started? What do you think I think?'

That is as close as an Iraqi could get in those days to showing disloyalty to the regime they both served and despised. And then he added something else. 'By the way, my son was born in Edinburgh. I was a postgraduate student at Heriot-Watt.'

When I was young I believed in the perfectibility of man, and in progress, and thought of journalism as a guiding light. If people were told the truth, if dishonour and injustice were clearly shown to them, they would at once demand the saving action, punishment of wrong-doers, and care for the innocent. How people were to accomplish these reforms, I did not know. That was their job. A journalist's job was to bring news, to be eyes for their conscience. I think I must have imagined public opinion as a solid force, something like a tornado, always ready to blow on the side of the angels.

(1998: 373)

I carried a similar delusion with me into the battlefields of the Balkans. For four years I sat in trenches, in basements, on front lines, in buildings under shellfire, on hillsides watching the fires of ethnic cleansing sweep away communities that had been planted there for generations, on checkpoints drinking homemade plum brandy from a warlord's hip flask. So much dishonour and injustice to report on: I think I too must have imagined public opinion as a solid force, something like a tornado, always ready to blow on the side of the angels.

Let me move you forward to the low watermark.

We had been standing around in the desert of northern Kuwait for most of the morning, getting dry and testy and each of us was coated with that thin film of fine, powdered sand that hangs in the air after a dust storm. It was March 2003. We were trying to get to Umm Qasr, in southern Iraq, courtesy of 4.2 Commando Royal Marines.

A friend of mine from the German television network ARD was having a rough time.

'German television?' the PR man from the British Army was saying. 'I'll tell you how much access the Germans can have. The same amount of access as you have troops on the ground.'

Sorry. No French, no Germans. Loyal journalists only. Or at least, journalists from belligerent nations only.

There is a description of a newsroom in *Scoop*, Evelyn Waugh's brilliant comic novel about war reporting. He defines it as a place 'where neurotic men in shirt sleeves and eye-shades rushed from telephone to tape machines, insulting and betraying one another in conditions of unredeemed squalor' (1938: 24). Update the equipment – satellite phones and laptop computers for telephones and tape machines – and Evelyn Waugh's newsroom has come to the desert.

We got to Umm Qasr eventually. But it was far from the front. The thunder of war had rolled north. Tales floated across the desert as snippets nascent political party, which used to meet in a little theatre called the Magic Lantern, was called Civic Forum. It was an assertion of the idea of Civil Society. It was a repudiation of despotism, of the arbitrary exercise of power by a self-perpetuating ruling elite.

Czech steelworkers marched out of the factory gates behind placards calling not for working-class solidarity, not for higher wages, not even for social justice, but for something much more fundamental. They walked behind placards proclaiming 'Plurality not Brutality'. They wanted what they could see the citizens of western Europe had and apparently took for granted – the right to remove their government at the ballot box; the rule of law; freedom under the law; the right to property and its protection under the law; plurality of opinion; the separation of church and state; free political and philosophical discourse.

The philosopher Ernest Gellner wrote about this just a few months before he died in 1995. Atlantic society, he wrote,

> is endowed with Civil Society, and on the whole, at any rate since 1945, it has enjoyed it without giving it much or any thought. Much contemporary social theory takes it for granted in an almost comical manner: ... Civil Society is simply presupposed as some kind of inherent attribute of the human condition! It is the corollary of a certain vision of man. It is a naïve universalisation of ONE rather fortunate KIND of man – the inhabitant of Civil Society. ... It is only the rediscovery of this ideal in Eastern Europe ... that has reminded the inhabitants of the liberal states on either shore of the northern Atlantic of just what it is that they possess and ought to hold dear.
>
> (1996: 13)

That moment on the square seems to me now to be some kind of high watermark. It was a time of hope for the world. It was also a time when it was easy for me to believe that there was some special virtue in this trade of ours, journalism. In Wenceslas Square people could see that I worked for the BBC. They came up to me to tell me how during the darkest days they had listened clandestinely to the corporation's Czech-language service; had played cat and mouse with the signal jammers in Moscow, chasing the frequencies up and down the dial.

In 1959, Martha Gellhorn, veteran reporter of the Spanish Civil War, the Second World War, Korea and countless Cold War proxy conflicts wrote this at about the stage in her reporting life that I think I must have reached now:

Foreword

Allan Little

There is a moment at which I was present as a reporter which has acquired in my mind the character of a fairy tale: I watched an old man change the world by uttering a single word. It was November 1989 and I was standing in a snow-flecked Wenceslas Square in Prague in what was then Czechoslovakia.

We emerged from the underground station. There were 400,000 people already there. We couldn't move. Vaclav Havel appeared from a window on a balcony above the crowd. And then, behind him, a slightly stooped, white-haired man whose face, to the crowd, was instantly recognisable, even though no photograph of him had been seen in public – in the newspapers or magazines, or on television – for twenty-one years. And then I heard an astonishing sound: it was the sound of breath being taken away. It was – in a literal sense – a breath-taking moment: 400,000 people gasping in disbelief. 'It's him', the young woman at my shoulder said. 'It's Dubcek.'

And when he stepped forward to the microphone he spoke one word, slowly and deliberately, its five syllables washing over us: 'CZESKOSLOVENSKO!' It struck me as interesting even then that after two decades of enforced silence the first word he chose to speak was not some abstract notion like 'liberty' or 'democracy', but something much more visceral, the name of the nation – the appeal of the tribe. At that moment, standing in the crisp, cold air of the square, you knew – everybody knew – that the genie was out of the bottle. Dubcek had spoken the word. What chance did the forty-year-old Soviet-imposed Communist regime stand? That night, about five or six hours after that moment, the Czechoslovak Politburo resigned. It was all over.

For the people of eastern and central Europe had for the most part long believed that a foreign tyranny had been imposed on them and had stood for four decades between them and their rightful destiny. And their rightful destiny was something that was easily expressed. Havel's

Acknowledgements

The idea for this book came from a conversation I had with Dr Sarah Niblock of Brunel University in the late summer of 2008, while I was still BBC Moscow correspondent. Both Dr Niblock, and her co-editor, Professor Julian Petley, have been most helpful during my research and writing. I am grateful too to Rebecca Barden and Paul Sng at Palgrave, and to my employers at London Metropolitan University for giving me time off from teaching in order to finish this book.

During my career as a journalist, I was fortunate enough to work with some very talented individuals and teams. I would like to make special mention of Fayed Abushammala for the invaluable assistance and advice he gave me when we worked together in Gaza. Andrew Kilrain and Linda Mottram, whom I met in Moscow in the 1990s, were always great company on the road, and true friends in time of need. All the bureau editors with whom I worked at the BBC: Sara Beck, Kevin Bishop, Andrew Steele, Andrew Roy, Jo Floto, Simon Wilson and Alan Quartly, were unfailingly supportive. I am grateful to the BBC's special correspondent, Allan Little, for countless conversations over the years which have helped me to form my ideas – not just about journalism, but about history, international relations and literature. Chris Booth's incisive and insightful reading of my draft has been a huge help. Thanks are also due to Patrick Garrett for his enthusiastic assistance with the index.

I am grateful to Irina Roberts at Andrew Nurnberg Associates for permission to quote from Vassily Grossman's *A Writer at War: Vassily Grossman with the Red Army 1941–1945* (2006).

Finally, I would like to mention my family: my parents, Margaret and Ian Rodgers, who have always encouraged me in my work, even when that involved going to places where few would wisely venture. My wife, Mette, is an outstanding foreign correspondent. It was our shared desire to see the world, and write about it, which led us to meet in Gaza. She, and our daughters, Freya and Sophia, bring me a joy that I never thought possible.

Contents

Acknowledgements   viii
Foreword Allan Little   ix

Introduction   1
1   From cavalry charges to citizen journalism – a brief
    history of conflict reporting   9
2   Access   28
3   Objectivity   46
4   How the war was spun: the role of public relations
    companies, propagandists and governments   66
5   Multi-platform storytelling   84
6   'Remember it's not your war': reporter involvement   102
7   Not as simple as 'death or glory': the future   121

Notes   139
References   142
Index   149

I understood that he understood more fully than I the nature, the value, the preciousness of Civil Society. And so, twelve years on, remembering that distant exchange, I sat in Kuwait waiting for the assault on Baghdad wondering where that same boy was now. He must be nineteen or twenty by now. I wondered whether he was on one of Saddam Hussein's front lines, under bombs from the country of his birth.

Information was part of the war effort. The Coalition War plan demanded that by the time US tanks reach the gates of Baghdad, the Iraqi regime would know – because they will have seen it on satellite television – that their authority had collapsed everywhere else in the country. What we report – the way we report it – is therefore a key part of the military campaign. The military have a term for it. They call it 'Information Operational Effect'.

In 1991 I had been on the other side – reporting the war from the enemy capital. For me it hadn't been 'Desert Storm', but the Iraqi leader's 'Mother of Battles'. We could not escape the fact that the Iraqis wanted us there – allowed us to be there – because they thought we would be useful to them. It was their version of Information Operational Effect.

These two episodes – Prague 1989, southern Iraq 2003 – book-end a changing world. In one, half a continent was reaching out to claim western values as their own; in the other a nation in the Arabian Gulf was having western values delivered to it on the back of an Abrams tank. In one a free media was celebrated as having contributed to something liberating; in the other that same media had to fight to extricate itself from round-the-clock manipulation, from Information Operational Effect.

Self-evidently, somewhere between 1989 and 2003 I stopped thinking of public opinion as a solid force, something like a tornado, always ready to blow on the side of the angels.

We're only journalists. Nothing we do will ever be perfect. We can only ever be the rough first draft of history. Why, if journalism cannot summon the tornado of public opinion to blow on the side of the angels, is it still worth it? This is Martha Gellhorn's answer to her own question: journalism is a means, she wrote, back in 1959,

> and I now think that the act of keeping the record straight is valuable in itself. Serious, careful, honest journalism is essential, not because it is a guiding light but because it is a form of honourable behaviour, involving the reporter and the reader.

> (1998: 373)

Of all the journalists I have worked with none has been more concerned with the business of getting it right than James Rodgers. When I worked with him first, in Boris Yeltsin's Russia, it struck me that what motivated him in keeping the record straight was a quiet but entrenched impulse to respect: respect for his audience, respect for his colleagues, above all respect for those on whose lives and (for the most part) misfortune, he was reporting. I admired that. I sought to emulate it. For those who agree to talk to you have made a decision to trust you with the story of their lives; they are trusting you to give a fair account of what they are living through. It is a kind of covenant.

James has written a thoughtful, carefully argued and at times highly affecting and very personal book about our trade. It is informed by his many years at the sharp end of news reporting, and by the hopes, excitements, fears and sorrows and exhilarations that go with it.

One counsel runs through this book like a thread through cloth: aspire, above all, to get it right. That's all.

Introduction

A superpower had broken up. War had broken out. In early January 1992, I flew from London to Moscow, and then on to Yerevan, capital of the newly independent republic of Armenia. From there, I took an overnight train journey to the Georgian capital, Tbilisi (this circuitous route from Moscow was the only way at the time – direct flights had ceased to operate) and arrived in the first of several conflict zones in which I was to work as a journalist.

The feelings and fears I experienced then are still vivid two decades later. I know that I was lucky in my early life. I was born and grew up in the affluent west, and, although as a teenager I was worried by the prospect of nuclear confrontation as the Cold War went through its menacing, final phase, the closest I ever came to experiencing armed conflict and its effects was in the tales of my grandparents, who remembered the Second World War, and in the history books that I loved to read as I child. So it was a shock to me, at the age of twenty-five, suddenly to find myself in the middle of a city where people were trying to kill each other; to hear gunfire which was not a cinema sound-effect, but the noise of one person seeking to end another's existence; to see the bodies, civilians among them, which were being taken for burial. For the first time, I saw the uniform of the warriors in the messy wars that were the conflicts of my time as a reporter: some bits of battledress, perhaps a tunic, or trousers, less frequently both, more often a tracksuit; ski hats more often than helmets; training shoes instead of army boots. It was the beginning of a time in Europe and beyond when many of those who went to war did so not in combat fatigues, but in leisurewear – a kind of deadly 'dress-down Friday', which did not end in a relaxing weekend, so much as stretch into the uncertain future. I remember drunken fighters in Tbilisi then, in front of the flame-blackened parliament, laughing as they reassured me that I had nothing to fear from their celebratory shooting.

In my career as a news journalist, I completed four foreign postings for the BBC: two in Moscow, one in Brussels and one in Gaza. I had already done one short posting to Moscow for Reuters Television before I joined the BBC. I also completed numerous other shorter assignments in Europe, the former Soviet Union, the Middle East and, following the attacks of September 11 2001, in the United States. I never thought of myself as a war correspondent, and I know few, if any, of my generation of journalists who would readily accept that description of what they do. The fact is that those of us who wanted to report on world affairs following the end of the Cold War could not easily confine ourselves to coverage of international politics and diplomacy. If we were to understand the way the world had started to work, we had to mix those stories with assignments that took us among the tracksuited warriors. Their emergence was perhaps unexpected to those of us who had rejoiced to see our nightmare of possible nuclear conflict end with the Cold War. Everyone was supposed to be free, and to be friends. It has not turned out that way, of course. Even if, as I write this in 2011, the Balkans and the Caucasus are quieter than they have been in the recent past, we need to understand what is happening in those places as never before. A few months earlier, I could have added the Middle East and North Africa to those 'quiet' places we need to understand. When the illusory calm ended in Egypt, Tunisia, Bahrain, Yemen, Libya and Syria our need for good journalism to help us understand why was clearly demonstrated. The prospects and progress of the wars between the tracksuited warriors – praised by some as heroes, and martyrs; reviled by their enemies as insurgents at best, more usually bandits and terrorists – and regular armies have not always been well understood or described. In this book, I will suggest how that can be changed.

When you work at the BBC, you are limited as to the personal views you can publicly express. I will disappoint any reader here who is expecting a former BBC journalist, now freed from the corporation's editorial constraints, to attack the organization which he formerly served. There are problems with the BBC, and with contemporary journalism in general, but listing them in order to allow my reader perhaps to infer that I had nothing to do with anything which is wrong is not my purpose. That there are things wrong with journalism today is not in itself news, even though I personally do not believe that, while there are good times and bad, there was ever a 'golden age' where all reporters were blessed with great intellect, limitless energy and irreproachable morals.

What I hope to do in writing this book is to try to offer a brief history of the way that covering conflict has evolved in the last twenty years, most particularly, but by no means exclusively, through my own personal experience. Where that experience is inferior to those of my contemporaries, I have looked to their accounts. This is a book that attempts to explain the practicalities of reporting conflict in order to help people to understand how their news is gathered and presented. Where there are faults and failings in that process, I hope to suggest ways in which they can be corrected. There are a lot of very good reporters in the world around us today, so, rather than simply listing what is wrong, I aim to emphasize what is good, and what can be even better.

Since the summer of 2010, I have been teaching journalism and media studies at London Metropolitan University. I am a relative newcomer to academia. My expertise in those fields is built on practical experience as a reporter, producer, presenter and editor, rather than as a lecturer and researcher. Still, I could not reasonably write this book without looking at some recent studies of the questions that I am seeking to address. As I am a newcomer to academia, I am also largely a newcomer to works that study journalism. Journalists do not generally read what academics write about them. Perhaps they should do so more, but that seems unlikely while working journalists have less and less time to do their job. While some studies written about conflict reporting offer insights which are truly illuminating, others are wide of the mark. David Morrison and Howard Tumber's book *Journalists at War: The Dynamics of News Reporting during the Falklands Conflict* (1988) is one I would put firmly in the illuminating category. But, as they themselves concede,

> Reading the academic literature one cannot help but feel sympathy with the journalists' claim that the 'outsider' has failed to get inside the trade: it is all too formalistic, too sterile, too serious; and it is not surprising, therefore, that working journalists fail to recognize the world they are supposed to inhabit. (1988: viii)

Good academic research, like good journalism, relies on good source material. Many of the people studying and researching journalism and the media in universities have limited experience of the working environment. That is particularly true of the area of journalism that I am writing about. While a researcher may be able to negotiate access to a newsroom or a TV production office in London, New York, Paris or elsewhere, it is hard to imagine the circumstances in which they could spend any useful length of time with a reporter covering a war. Much of academics' understanding of the field of reporting conflict – not perhaps the editorial decision-making in head office, but the process of newsgathering – is therefore by its nature secondhand, and consequently limited. I hope, as a journalist turned journalism lecturer, to use my experience of the two worlds to try to bring a rare and informed perspective to my subject.

Since I became a journalist in the early 1990s, the world's political power blocs have cracked and shifted. Technology has evolved in ways we could not have imagined then. Those political and technological changes have both had massive influence on the way in which conflicts have arisen, and been fought. The changes have been mirrored, too, in the way in which we report those conflicts. The tracksuited warriors' battles have been covered not only by the conventional reporter working for large news organizations such as Reuters and the BBC, but also by the 'citizen journalist' and blogger: war correspondents as far removed from traditional journalistic structures as their subjects are from traditional chains of military command.

The big media organizations have had to respond to these changes. Their previous dominance over newsgathering and distribution has fractured and diminished like the structures of power from the Cold War era. Relatively cheap mobile technology has raised 'user-generated content' (UGC) – material provided by people who would traditionally have been members of the audience rather than contributors – to the status of an important force in news broadcasting. In one sense, this is not entirely new. As soon as home video cameras became common, in wealthy countries at least, reporters arriving at the scene of a transport or natural disaster would make it their priority to find out if there were any 'amateur video' available of the actual event, the aftermath of which they had been assigned to cover. Now, such material is increasingly frequently available. Where 'amateur video' relied on the 'amateur' having the presence of mind to grab their camera and seize the moment, now they will have their camera with them all the time. It is in the mobile phone, which they can then use to send their material straight to the broadcaster or agency, possibly before the scoop-hunting reporter or producer has even had the chance to ask them for it. UGC has become an unprecedented source of exclusive material, and, less welcome, a whole new area of opportunity for the hoaxer and copyright thief. Still, it is one leading example of the way that major news organizations have had to respond to changes which they cannot control. Does not the phrase 'user-generated content' sound much more respectful than 'amateur video'? Even when UGC looks bad on screen, the broadcaster is usually too polite – or too mindful of the fact that ultimately it is they who put it there – to say so.

Newspapers all over the world now supply their content – often free

– to internet users. Broadcasters distribute theirs on social networking and microblogging sites: platforms over which they have no control. The distinction between newspaper and broadcaster is now blurred, in highly developed media markets, at least. Here in Britain, the national newspapers' websites provide extensive audio and video content, which they proudly promote in their printed paper editions. The BBC and Sky News websites offer text versions of the stories which they broadcast.

As those distinctions between what news organizations do, between who provides material for which platforms, become less clear, so too does the idea of who is a journalist. In the era of the tracksuited warrior with a mobile phone, the definitions of combatant, civilian and reporter are less clear. People in conflict zones may be seen to belong to more than one of those groups. One of my interviewees for this book, Major Richard Streatfeild of the British Army, was both a commander and a reporter during a tour of duty in Afghanistan from 2009–10. When we spoke, he did not feel that 'officer-journalist' accurately described his role. Even so, it did combine those two ideas, and the news media will have to find ways not only to see what opportunities insights like his represent, but also ways to use them to their best effect. More controversially for mainstream media, I would suggest that that involves more effort trying to gather and report the views of the enemies of conventional armies too. Governments who refuse to talk to those they call 'terrorists' invariably portray their position as one of the highest principle, which will enable them to win through in the end. Just as invariably, they are often talking to their 'terrorist' enemies in secret at the same time. The British government spoke to the IRA in private before they did so in public; at the time of writing the outgoing US Secretary of Defense has just confirmed that talks with the Taliban are ongoing. The history of the second half of the twentieth century, and into our own, is full of examples where states have had to accept that negotiating with those they find unacceptable is inevitable. They have to be included in the process.

I would argue that they have to be included in complete, competent journalism too. That is not a new idea, but it has not been happening enough recently. If more effort had been made to question the conventional wisdom that the US and its allies' invasion of Iraq in 2003 was destined for great success, tens of thousands of Iraqi civilians might have been spared. After the invasion, the bloggers in occupied Iraq emerged as new and highly informative voices. This was particularly true at a time when non-Iraqi journalists, especially those from countries whose troops were among the invaders, were often unable to work properly because they feared for their own safety. These are the kind of voices that increasingly need to be heard. Neither the bloggers, nor Major Streatfeild, could have done what they did without digital technology. Now more and more people can, and should.

Where does this leave the conventional war correspondent? It puts them at risk of redundancy, but with the possibility of redeployment. For a moment, let us leave them at the corner of the hotel bar where popular legend placed them on most evenings of the twentieth century.

One line that inspired me to write this book, and which has never been far from my thoughts as I have done so, comes from Michael Herr's *Dispatches*. He was writing almost four decades ago about his experience in Vietnam, but his clearly expressed conclusions about that conflict are applicable to countless others, 'Conventional journalism could no more reveal this war than conventional firepower could win it' (1977: 175).

Dispatches was first published in 1975. In the intervening years, 'conventional journalism' has only sometimes succeeded in revealing the wars it reported. It may now be possible to improve that. Reporting is the first rough draft of history, as Philip Graham, the former publisher of the *Washington Post* is usually credited with saying. The phrase 'rough draft' implies that a better draft may come later, but the first may be the one which has the greatest influence on forming contemporary opinion. Also in *Dispatches* Herr accepts that, as a magazine rather than a daily news journalist he 'never had to run back to any bureau or office to file' (ibid.: 171). So while we must praise his achievement in creating an account of war reporting that remains influential to this day, it is the work of his modern-day counterparts in continuous news (daily news now seems too outdated a concept – deadlines fall far more frequently) with which we are concerned here.

Overview

Reporting Conflict begins with a short history of the way that journalists have worked in wartime, the latter part concentrating on my own experience since the early 1990s. My purpose here is to try to explain briefly how the role of the journalist in wartime was first defined, subsequently developed and how the pace of that development has quickened in recent years. Because it seems a natural departure point for the rest of the book, I have chosen access as the subject of Chapter 2. My purpose is to demonstrate to journalist and non-journalist readers alike the way in which access, or lack of it, to locations and information, shapes the way a reporter works. Chapter 3 develops the idea of a journalist at work by focusing on the concept of objectivity. It looks at Martin Bell's notion of a journalism of attachment (Bell, 1995), and also at the work of Anna Politkovskaya, a brave and determined reporter, whose work, like that of her compatriot Vassily Grossman, whose war reporting I also refer to at various points during the book, I feel has not received its due international recognition. In Chapter 3, I also analyse my experience of reporting on the capture of Saddam Hussein in 2003 – particularly for the way in which the occupying powers sought to manage it as a propaganda event.

Expanding on ideas of journalism and propaganda, Chapter 4 looks at the role of public relations companies as they seek to influence the way in which conflict is reported. My principal research here is based on the 2008 war between Russia and Georgia, which I covered, and about which David Edmonds and I subsequently made a BBC radio documentary, *The PR Battle for the Caucasus* (Rodgers and Edmonds, 2008). The resources which the belligerents poured into spinning that war were, in my experience, without precedent. The role played by hired consultants should be more widely known for the effect it has on audiences' understanding.

This is especially an issue in the world of twenty-four-hour news, so Chapter 5 looks at the particular pressures that newsgathering for multi-platform, round-the-clock distribution has brought to conflict reporting. Here I will draw on my experiences of working in the Gaza Strip during the second Palestinian *intifada*, and in South Ossetia just after the 2008 war. From the pressures arising from changing technology, I turn to the personal factors that can influence the coverage of conflict. Chapter 6, 'Remember It's Not Your War', looks at what motivates reporters, and develops further ideas of objectivity, especially as they relate to the way in which journalists work when their own families and property are threatened by the conflict that they are covering. My main focus here is Israel's military assault on the Gaza Strip, which began in December 2008. My concluding chapter, Chapter 7, I have called 'Not as Simple as "Death or Glory"' to reflect the need for conflict journalism that does not shy away from trying to explain complex issues. In this chapter, I bring together my ideas from earlier sections of the book to try to suggest ways in which conflict journalism can tackle the challenge represented by this complexity.

There are issues and places that I do not feel able to address, or at least to the extent that they might merit. The conflicts I have considered in detail are those of which I have firsthand experience, so I do not cover Congo, Darfur, the drug wars of Colombia or Mexico. Afghanistan is not dealt with in detail for the same reason, although I would argue that my ideas are relevant to the coverage of that country. Nor have I written about journalists and post-traumatic stress disorder; journalists' use of armed security guards while on assignment; or analysed at length the use of language in covering conflict. All of these are important topics which are omitted here only for reasons of space.

Let us return now to the conventional war reporter. As Richard Sambrook noted in a paper on foreign correspondents, published for the Reuters Institute for the Study of Journalism in December 2010, economics, globalization and new technology are changing the way that international news is gathered and distributed. The huge amount of news sources now available – irrespective of their actual worth – means that it is harder for the conventional foreign correspondent to exist. Eyewitness reporting, and expertise, have not, however, fallen in value. On the contrary, they are becoming more valuable. While we have to recognize the significance and importance of UGC, it is not enough on its own. As Richard Evans, a colleague at London Metropolitan University asked rhetorically when giving a lecture on 'citizen journalism', 'You would not trust a citizen dentist, so why trust a citizen journalist?' The conflicts of the future will be complicated, multi-sided, and shaped, as always, by politics and technology. The reporting that describes them will be, too.

1 From cavalry charges to citizen journalism – a brief history of conflict reporting

The journalist working in wartime is a figure who has been lionized, satirized and despised. Reporters covering conflict seem to hold a special place in the public perception of journalism: at times, they are seen as brave and noble, at others, foolhardy and self-serving. Although accounts of combat are as old as war itself, it was not until the nineteenth century that the kind of conflict reporting we are used to today first emerged. William Howard Russell, *The Times* correspondent in the Crimea, is often considered one of the first, if not the first, war correspondents. He has a much less well-known namesake, James Russell, who might now also be considered a trailblazer. James Russell was a Searjent[1] Major in the Scots Grays at the Battle of Waterloo. The day after what he called 'a most Bloody Battle with the French as ever was fought', he wrote a letter to his family to let them know that he had survived. I will look at this letter and the wider significance of correspondence like it in greater detail towards the end of the chapter, but I choose it as a starting point because it not only predates what we have come to think of as the conventional model of war reporting, but also includes some of the great techniques of that model – compelling narrative, detail and an awareness of the wider strategic picture – and anticipates some of the kinds of war reporting that are beginning to influence the one to which we have become accustomed.

Recent studies of conflict reporting, such as Piers Robinson *et al.*'s *Pockets of Resistance: British News Media, War, and Theory in the 2003 Invasion of Iraq* (2010), have tended to analyse the finished product, without always considering the process of newsgathering in the kind of detail offered by journalists' memoirs. While Phillip Knightley's *The First Casualty* (1989) remains unsurpassed as a history of journalism in wartime, it predates the end of the Cold War, and the attacks of

September 11 2001. Susan Carruthers's impressive *The Media at War*, recently updated (2011), includes a detailed assessment of that period but does not give the reader enough of a sense of primary newsgathering, the daily work of reporters, work that is continually evolving, but which remains the most important part of the process. Morrison and Tumber's *Journalists at War* – their account of the coverage of the Falklands conflict of 1982 – examines that process in detail, and is still invaluable reading today, but has now been overtaken by new wars, and new technology. My approach will be to try to fill in those gaps by drawing on my own experience as a journalist, the accounts of other journalists, and with reference to existing academic studies.

The forces that shape journalism in wartime can be divided into three broad categories: personal, political and technological. The personal ones are those which affect the journalist in the place where they are working: access; the company in which they find themselves; and the journalist's own involvement in the action. The history of conflict reporting shows that there are two further factors above all others that have shaped it beyond the personal level: politics, and technology. Professional ideas of objectivity and ethics are also important, and fit into the personal and political categories. Throughout this book, politics and technology will be the factors to which I will return in order to explain how conflict reporting works now, and how it is likely to work in the future. By politics, I mean the international political and diplomatic situation at any given time. I take this in the widest possible sense, to include, naturally, economic factors, but also social ones, such as cultural and religious attitudes. These decide which conflicts arise, who is drawn into them, who needs to know about them, and who tries to influence the way that information is or is not distributed. This was as true for William Howard Russell as it has been for me and my contemporaries who have covered conflict in the post-Cold War, post-September 11 world.

William Howard Russell was as a pioneer because he was an *observer*, not a combatant or civilian taking part in the action voluntarily or otherwise. Russell was a civilian who went to a conflict zone specifically to relay his account of what was happening there back to an audience[2] in another place. He did this in the Crimean War of the 1850s. Britain and France, bitter enemies some four decades earlier when James Russell was fighting, had become allies against Russia (Figes, 2010). William Howard Russell cannot, perhaps, be considered a fully neutral observer: he was working for a newspaper, *The Times*, which had enormous influence on public opinion and policy in the home country of one of the belligerents. His use of the first-person plural, 'we', 'us' and 'our', would jar with some modern ideas of the reporter's impartiality but they do have their contemporary equivalent in the 'our boys' that some British newspapers have used much more recently to describe British troops. Nevertheless, Russell's presence as a witness, rather than an actor – he was neither a combatant nor a local resident – marks his as a new role. More importantly for what followed, it defined the model of the war correspondent which would endure for the rest of the nineteenth century, through the twentieth and into our own. His reporting is not only remembered because of its historical significance. It has lasted because it still reads so well today, more than a century and a half later. Take his account of the disastrous charge of the Light Cavalry Brigade:

> At ten minutes past eleven, our Light Cavalry Brigade advanced. As they rushed towards the front, the Russians opened on them from the guns in the redoubt on the right with volleys of musketry and rifles. They swept proudly past, glittering in the morning sun in all the pride and splendour of war.
>
> (2008: 127)

There follows a detailed and dramatic description of the action, which ends with massive losses, before Russell asks us to glance again at his watch, and see how many casualties have been suffered in how little a time: 'At thirty-five minutes past eleven, not a British soldier, except the dead and dying, was left in front of these bloody Muscovite guns' (ibid.: 128).

Describing the aftermath of a later action in the campaign, Russell shows his skill in one of the arts of the great reporter: creating a sense of place, of action, which brings the audience, however far physically removed, almost to his side, to see what he sees:

> It was agonizing to see the wounded men who were lying there under a broiling sun, parched with excruciating thirst, racked with fever, and agonized with pain – to behold them waving their caps faintly, or making signals towards our lines, over which they could see the white flag waving.
>
> (ibid.: 220)

The contrast with the description higher up of the 'pride and splendour of war' is striking. Russell's portrayal of this side of death and conflict – no heroic death here, just unimaginable suffering – is one that finds echoes in the work of many of those who followed his example in later years, and went to wars to write about them.

War is more than anything a terribly squalid business. On the wireless or in a paper it appears clear-cut, a question of strategy, gains and losses. Here you see files of hang-dog prisoners, churches, farmhouses, cottages, mined and passed over, where tanks have come to grips and men died by the hundred.

(Moynihan, 1994: 62)

So wrote Michael Moynihan in *War Correspondent*, his account of reporting on some of the most decisive battles of the Second World War. The words 'on the wireless or in a paper' seem outdated in our multi-platform world but the sentiment endures. Those of us who have tried to describe conflict in our reporting have all experienced this sense of squalor, and how it contrasts with statements of advances, and clinical destruction of enemies, issued by suited prime ministers or immaculately uniformed staff officers in the controlled environments of governmental news conferences. That contrast has always been one of the main challenges facing the professional reporter whose task it has been to convey the action to an audience near or far, in danger, or just interested. Since the 1850s, when William Howard Russell rose to fame, that task has largely been carried out in a way which he himself would readily recognize – in approach, if not in technology.

From the Crimea to the Second World War

Increasing literacy and better transport meant that newspapers' circulation grew as the nineteenth century progressed. For Britain, an expanding empire brought a desire and a need to learn of distant conflicts for the way in which they had an impact on life at home: politics and technology shaped newsgathering and distribution as they do today. The First World War brought troops from the far corners of that empire to fight in Flanders and France. Correspondents came too. That war also changed the way in which western Europe understood conflict. Aerial bombardments and machine guns – the mechanical horrors of war in the twentieth century – crushed ideas of heroic cavalry charges. Those reporters who did travel to the battlefields to relay events back to the population at home enjoyed the benefits of ever-improving communications, but also fell victim to censorship: some they had imposed on them by governments; some they willingly consented to provide themselves (Knightley, 1989; Carruthers, 2011). These ideas of technological advance and editorial control continued to develop side by side (Schneider, 2011: 32), often competing against each other as they do to this day (Robinson *et al.*, 2010: 29). There was enormous social change too – nowhere more than on the other side of Europe from the mud of Flanders, in Russia. The Russian revolution was chronicled by western correspondents – among them, the future children's author, Arthur Ransome (Chambers, 2009) – who witnessed events that would shape the entire twentieth century.

It was Ransome's contemporary, John Reed, though, who has left us the most famous journalistic account of the time when Russia tore apart its old order as it sought to create a new world. John Reed was a foreigner, an American, yet he believed passionately in the ideals of the Bolsheviks who took power and set up the Soviet state. His *Ten Days That Shook the World* (1977) is the story of an armed struggle for power, which was not a conventional war, and, as such, even though it tells the story of a revolution that happened almost a century ago, it contains many lessons that are relevant today: ideas of objectivity, freedom of the press, a reporter's purpose and propaganda. John Reed's experiences and techniques would have been readily recognized by William Howard Russell, half a century before. They also seem familiar to me and my contemporaries, who began our careers in the 1990s, covering the collapse of the system whose birth Reed himself recorded. He seeks to witness as much himself as he can and, when events conspire against him, he finds the people who were there to help him complete his story. There is a reminder of the role that reporters themselves play when Reed sees the following scene in the streets of St Petersburg: 'a man appeared with an armful of newspapers, and was immediately stormed by frantic people, offering a rouble, five roubles, ten roubles, tearing at each other like animals' (1977: 95).

Reed himself is dismissive of what the 'frantic people' end up with: he calls it 'a feverish little sheet of four pages, containing no news' (ibid.: 95–6). It is nevertheless a moment when the correspondent in the middle of a conflict is shown the value of journalism itself. When I was covering the war in Chechnya in 1995 and later, we western reporters used to carry cigarettes, chocolate and other small gifts to help break the ice with combatants. What Russian soldiers wanted most of all, though, were newspapers – and a ten-day-old copy of a national paper from Moscow was considered a great prize.

In the Second World War, troops were sent across the world to different theatres of combat, and correspondents went with them. Advances in technology had facilitated the broadcasting process, increasing its importance. Radio became the medium with the greatest influence: think of wartime addresses by leaders designed to inspire suffering and fearful nations, think of the propaganda each belligerent used to undermine the morale of the enemy's population. With the sense that many nations were fighting for their very survival, with the sense that going to war with Nazi Germany was a moral obligation, this was a time when few correspondents tried to adhere to traditional notions of objectivity (Carruthers, 2011: 78, 129). It seemed out of place against a foe that many considered the greatest evil, and greatest threat to Europe, in the twentieth century, and perhaps of all time. There was a sense in which this was used to legitimize censorship. As Asa Briggs wrote in *The BBC: The First Fifty Years*, 'Censorship, according to the American journalist Quentin Reynolds, who was to make a reputation later as a broadcaster, was "petty, absurd, tyrannical"' (1985: 178). Still, as Briggs also notes, this did not pose a major ethical dilemma for BBC staff, working under threat of Nazi invasion.

> Indeed while the Battle of Britain lasted, BBC staff felt themselves to be in the front line, carrying out essential war duties and ensuring that, unlike the German broadcasting system, where on a bad day most German transmitters were off the air, 'we never closed'.
>
> (ibid.: 194)

If in this case the issue of moral judgement and how it might apply to professional ethics was easily resolved, it serves to illustrate a question which almost every journalist covering conflict has had to consider at one time or another: who is in the right here, and how should that be reflected in my reporting?

Access and objectivity

For Vassily Grossman, covering the Second World War for *Krasnaya Zvezda* ('Red Star' – the newspaper of the Soviet Army) – this was no dilemma demanding lengthy consideration. As well as a committed believer in the Soviet system, Grossman was Jewish. The town where his mother lived had been occupied by the Nazis relatively early in the war. As he reports from the fighting, in the thick of all the horrors of the eastern front, he allows himself to wonder what might have happened to his mother. However tireless, dedicated and, in Grossman's case, unfailingly brilliant, a combat reporter may be, there are moments when he or she has also to reflect that they remain a human being, a citizen, a daughter or a son. Grossman has one such moment of personal emotion when he is following the Red Army westwards, as it drives back the invader, and he pauses to think of his mother,

No I don't believe she is still alive. I travel all the time around areas that have been liberated, and I see what these accursed monsters have done to old people and children. And Mama was Jewish. A desire to exchange my pen for a rifle is getting stronger and stronger in me.

(2006: 224)

When the correspondent is unquestioningly patriotic, as Grossman was at that time, his or her work poses little challenge to the authorities. When the aims of the party in conflict are at odds with the purpose of the reporter, tension inevitably arises (Morrison and Tumber, 1988: 21, 44; Carruthers, 2011: 56). Each army in each war has tried to refine the relationship it wants to have with journalists, and the result has been everything from 'you can do what you like but careful you keep out of our way', through varying degrees of control, to total denial of access. Each approach has been examined both at the time and subsequently as a success or a failure, a model to discard, or one to use again in the future. These issues will be examined in greater detail in the next chapter, but the question of differing purpose between army and reporter takes us to the next milestone in the history of war reporting: Vietnam. If the Second World War saw the rise of radio to the height of influence, Vietnam was the first war extensively seen on television (Hallin, 1989: 105), just as the Iraq war of 1991 has often been described as the first war on *live* television (Thussu, 2003: 118).

Edward S. Herman and Noam Chomsky devote a large part of their influential work *Manufacturing Consent* to a consideration of the way that the news media, and television in particular, may or may not have influenced the outcome of the Vietnam War. 'The standard critique of the media for having "lost the war" identifies television as the major culprit,' (1994: 199) is how Herman and Chomsky succinctly define an argument which they challenge at length. Instead, they suggest, the US media 'were so closely wedded to U.S. government goals that they never sought to learn the facts' (ibid.: 194). In *The 'Uncensored War'*, Daniel Hallin concludes that, 'The collapse of America's "will" to fight in Vietnam resulted from a political process of which the media were only part' (1989: 213) – divisions in public and political opinion being reflected in coverage, rather than formed by it. All the same, this 'belief that the media, particularly television, were responsible for U.S. government failures' (Herman and Chomsky, 1994: 170) made such a big impression that Carruthers, writing of the Gulf War in 1991, found it still stubbornly in existence, even though, as she notes, 'As in previous wars, the presumed power of images to shatter morale may have been more important than their actual effect' (2000: 142). I will consider the work of Hallin and Herman and Chomsky on Vietnam in greater detail in Chapter 4, but, to conclude here, there are, in essence, two views: one holds that television reporting of the Vietnam War played a hugely important role in shaping public opinion, a public opinion which, informed about the war, ceased to support US military presence in Vietnam – with the result that the war effort was undermined to the extent that it failed. Others dismiss this as an attempt to deflect the blame from politicians, diplomats and generals and onto the news media. However one sees it, politics affected the way in which the war was reported.

Technology did too. Advances in the distribution of television pictures permitted moving images of the conflict to be brought into the lives of non-combatants thousands of miles away on an unprecedented scale. Audiences started to become used to sitting in their favourite armchair and watching pictures from the thick of the fighting which had only recently been filmed (Sontag, 2003: 18). The emphasis that has been placed on television coverage, though, should not be allowed to eclipse that of journalists working in other media. Some of the most enduring, and, even at this distance, still troubling, images are the work of stills photographers; some of the strongest words spoken not over pictures and sound of battle, but committed to the printed page. The pictures taken by Don McCullin, Tim Page and others still make an impression. McCullin's 'grunt (infantryman) suffering severe shell shock' (1992: 110) is one such. Even now, more than three decades after publication, Michael Herr's *Dispatches* still conveys an unforgettable sense of what it was like to witness the conflict, and what it was like to write about it. His passage about the way that covering the Tet offensive made him feel still defines the combination of emotion and sensation the reporter documenting conflict can experience, an example of the personal factors I mentioned above:

Tet was pushing correspondents closer to the wall than they'd ever wanted to go. I realized later that, however childish I might remain, actual youth had been pressed out of me in just the three days that it took me to cross the sixty miles between Can Tho and Saigon. In Saigon, I saw friends flipping out almost completely; a few left, some took to their beds for days with the exhaustion of deep depression. I went the other way, hyper and agitated, until I was only doing three hours of sleep a night. A friend on the *Times* said he didn't mind his nightmares so much as the waking impulse to file on them.

(1977: 63)

While it is true that Herr's striking work can still command our attention today, there is no doubt that Vietnam marked a time when television took another big step forward in securing its dominance over how the mass audience learns about conflict. It was not until the early 1990s that there was a similar, seminal, change.

War twenty-four

In January 1991, a military coalition led by the United States attacked Iraq. The purpose of the assault was to force Saddam Hussein to withdraw his forces from Kuwait, which they had invaded the previous August. As the first missiles landed on the Iraqi capital, Baghdad, CNN's correspondent, Peter Arnett, who had reported on the Vietnam War, was there – broadcasting live from his hotel. This was not live TV from a war zone as we have come to know it in the intervening two decades. Much of the reporting that night was on the phone. The round-the-clock hotel-rooftop shot of the correspondent reporting live in flak jacket and helmet had yet to evolve, but this was the night that prepared audiences for its arrival. As such, it was a new departure: one in which a technology-led change altered the way wars would be reported, and audience expectations, for good. The entry into conflict reporting of round-the-clock television news also had political consequences for the way in which it would force governments to structure their own media policies (for a detailed case study of government wartime media strategies in the age of twenty-four-hour news, see Chapter 4), and for the way it would affect news organizations' own ways of working. Some years later, Daya Kishan Thussu wrote, '"24/7 News" (24-hour news, 7 days a week) has emerged as a television genre in its own right' (2003: 117). This was one of the most significant nights in that process (or perhaps, from Jean Baudrillard's point of view, the night when war began watching 'itself in a mirror' (2009: 31).

The BBC interrupted its scheduled programming to rebroadcast CNN. By doing so, it was in effect admitting that it had failed to anticipate a sea change in international journalism. Its decision to air CNN's pictures, though, did at least show that the BBC understood the significance of what CNN was doing. Not long afterwards, the BBC itself entered the arena of continuous news, starting by using one of its radio frequencies to broadcast coverage of the war. Cynics inside and outside the corporation named it 'Scud FM' in reference to the missiles used by the Iraq forces and that featured so frequently in news reports.

New wars, and new questions for journalism

As the 1990s went on, satellite newsgathering (SNG) became cheaper and more versatile. The wars in the former Yugoslavia from 1991 onwards were the starting point for a new generation of correspondents who had grown up during the Cold War, and were now reporting on the conflicts that had erupted with the passing of old certainties. Their tasks, as they did so, were made easier by the increasing use of satellite telephones, and SNG equipment which could be packed up into a few boxes – for this was the time when, inspired by the example of CNN's coverage of the 1991 Gulf War, broadcasters were looking for all the live reporting they could get. This was not a development that was universally welcomed. As Thussu, for example, has claimed, 'one result of these developments is that conflict reporting tends towards infotainment' (Thussu, 2003: 117). There were other concerns too. For people in Britain and, through the BBC's international radio and television channels, around the world, Martin Bell became the reporter most readily identified with covering the conflict in Bosnia. In his memoir, *In Harm's Way: Reflections of a War Zone Thug*, published in 1995, he describes a colleague so snowed under by requests for live reports that 'he hardly had time to pick up the phone and talk to the UN spokesman' (1995: 29). This question of the relative time allocated to newsgathering and reporting continues to press today, and I will discuss it in greater detail in Chapter 5. But *In Harm's Way* is remembered more for an ethical debate rather than for an issue raised by changing technology. This was a time of new international politics, which, in Bell's view, raised new editorial challenges. 'Twenty-five years of reporting other wars weren't helping me with this one' (ibid.: 19), Bell says as he recalls his arrival in

April 1992. But what he saw there – particularly the fate of civilians –
led him to argue that some of the reporting was failing. 'In the news
business it isn't involvement but indifference that makes for bad practice,' he wrote later. 'Good journalism is the journalism of *attachment*'
(ibid.: 127–8).

In a sense, this was not a new issue. It had been raised previously
both in fiction and journalistic debate. In Graham Greene's novel *The
Quiet American*, Thomas Fowler, a British journalist caught up in death
and intrigue in Indochina before the Vietnam War, takes pride in his
complete detachment, to the point where he could definitely be
accused of what Bell calls 'indifference'. What was new was Bell's challenge to the accepted orthodoxy. Especially among reporters from the
English-speaking world, and especially, among them, for television and
radio journalists, objectivity – even to the point of 'indifference' – was
best practice. It was, the conventional wisdom held, the only practice
worth adopting. In the bloodshed that followed the end of
Communism in Europe, Bell advanced an argument for a new approach
in new times. It is a debate that continues today, as journalists are
increasingly faced with conflicts that do not fit into the conventional
state-against-state or army-against-army categories which defined our
earlier understanding of war. If in their causes the conflicts in the
former Yugoslavia in the 1990s can in some ways be seen as a continu-
ation of the Second World War, the challenge they represented for journalists was very much of its own time: fought in urban areas, where
civilians were targets as well as combatants, and where the distinction
between the two was not always clear.

Case study: access to information, and 'telling the truth' in a civil war: Georgia 1992

A few months before Martin Bell arrived in Bosnia with his twenty-five
years' experience of covering conflict, I arrived in Tbilisi, the capital of
Georgia, for my first assignment to a war zone. Georgia had become
independent from Moscow just months earlier, with the collapse of the
Soviet Union. Now there was civil war between rival groups seeking to
control the fledgling country: a conflict which was characteristic of the
post-Cold War world in which I began my career as a journalist. The
Soviet Union, one of the power blocs that had dominated the world in
which I had grown up, had formally ceased to exist only a few days
before. The sense of vanished certainty, of a system which had just

disappeared, was felt at every level. One of the first things that a journalist usually thinks about on arrival in a conflict zone is getting accreditation. A press card can be invaluable in assisting with gaining access, in explaining your way out of a hostile or potentially dangerous confrontation – especially where there is no common language – even, in extreme examples of the latter, instrumental in saving your life. There, in Tbilisi, in January 1992, it was not at all clear who might have the authority to issue such a pass, so there was no point in seeking it out. A press card from the just-defunct Soviet foreign ministry in Moscow was the best document to have – that, or an identity card from an international employer. In my case that was Visnews, an international television news agency, which was later to become Reuters Television.

The day after I arrived in Georgia, the enemies of the then leader, Zviad Gamsakhurdia, drove him from power. They celebrated their victory on the steps of the parliament building in Tbilisi's main thoroughfare by firing into the air and toasting their success with swigs of strong alcohol. Weapons alone, rather than military dress or discipline, distinguished combatant from bystander. The evening before, from a hotel up on a hillside overlooking the city centre, I had my first experience of watching tracer fire in the night sky as the warring sides took the coming of darkness as a cue to resume fighting. It was my first experience of a combat zone, and my first experience of the issues to which I referred above, and which I will discuss in greater detail later in the book: access, objectivity, outside influences and the journalist's personal involvement in the action and the way it is related.

The first challenge was simply to understand what was going on. From Herman and Chomsky's propaganda model (1994: 1) onwards, there has been a tendency in academia to see shortcomings in reporting conflict as a kind of conspiracy. Sometimes, though, in cases like Georgia, reporting can be inaccurate simply because reporters are fallible, or do not have the full facts. The number of factions I found in Georgia – after years of official suppression of nationalist and other movements, it seemed almost every political or ethnic group was seeking self-determination – perhaps mirrors Martin Bell's impressions on arriving in Bosnia where his experience of other wars seemed of little help. In any case, there was a lot to learn and no obviously reliable source of information. In the same way that the Communist bloc had fractured in the years preceding the Georgian civil war, countries within that bloc had split too. The absence of any clear authority, and, in this case, such authority as there was changing within twenty-four hours of my arrival, meant that there was very little in the way of official information. Official information can be just one-sided propaganda, and often is in wartime. But it is at least a starting point in the journalist's attempt to interpret events which she or he can only partially see. Until you arrive in a conflict zone for the first time, you cannot fully appreciate how obscured and incomplete your view of the action is likely to be. On that occasion, the difficulties and danger involved in travelling far from the capital made it impossible to give a comprehensive picture of the war across the whole of the country – so the international media's experiences, and therefore the understanding of its audiences, were confined to a fairly narrow area of Tbilisi.

One single day's reporting, focusing on one single incident, illustrates these and other difficulties the journalist encounters daily in a conflict zone.

Supporters of the ousted leader, Zviad Gamsakhurdia, began to gather outside the railway station to show their support for Mr Gamsakhurdia, and to demand that he be returned to power. This was the age before the internet connected activist to journalist. To make sure that the international media were aware of their plans, the night before their first rally, the demonstrators arrived at the hotel where most of the foreign press were staying to shout their intention up at the windows. The next day, the cameraman I was working with and I duly made our way to the square in front of the station. Here we had to take our first important decision. Even if the battle for the capital a day or two before appeared decisive, there was still a danger that those newly in charge would not permit the demonstration to go ahead. There was every chance that the protesters would be fired upon by their enemies. Editorial priorities, especially for television, suggested that it would be best to be down on the square, right in the thick of the action. A sense of safety, and frankly, of fear, suggested it would be much better to be somewhere far less exposed. If the demonstration did provoke shooting, the attackers would be likely to fire where the crowd was thickest. We decided to go down into the square for a short while. I did my best to look around for any approaching threat while my colleague's vision was narrowed to what he was filming at any one time.

Nearby, the experience of a newspaper correspondent from the United States illustrated the issue of external influence and pressure, in a very direct way. Members of the crowd, themselves knowing that they could be shot at any moment, and therefore very tense, were asking him if he wrote 'the truth'. He did his best to explain how he understood his role. The exchange of views was not made any easier by the fact that it was conducted in Russian: the first language of neither the reporter nor his interlocutors. 'I just write "he said this" and "'the other said that",' he said. This did not satisfy the demonstrators. For them, any reflection of their enemies' views was not objectivity so much as the willing reporting of lies. The reporter mollified his critics sufficiently to allow him to move away and continue his work at a safer distance – but the lesson was clear: those who were directly involved in the conflict saw anyone present as a protagonist of one sort or another. This is where the role of a reporter as a propagandist such as John Reed was, or even as a committed patriot, such as Vassily Grossman, can be much more straightforward. Their presence in the war zone is part of a drive to promote a particular political and/or military cause. As my colleague from the US discovered, many of the protagonists see reporters in this way in any case.

We waited while the protesters assembled, listened to some speeches, started to move off. We had a deadline approaching. We had to leave to send our material. Satellite transmission time then was short and expensive. If you missed the ten-minute slot booked for you to send your material, you would have wasted very precious time, and at least $1,000. Our interpretation of what was happening was controlled by the constraints of the technology with which we were working. On that occasion, it turned out to be a major problem. Somewhere along the route of the march, the demonstrators' enemies lay in wait. They opened fire, killing a number of the protesters. By leaving to send our earlier – already outdated, and not especially strong, material – my colleague and I had missed the most important event of the day. It served to reinforce my realization that the conflict reporter will always be confined to a partial view of the whole picture, like a spectator at a chess match who is only permitted to see some of the squares on the board – especially when they are tied to fixed deadlines, at fixed locations.

Mobile technology and its implications for journalist and audience: Iraq 2003 and Gaza 2009

Since then, the pace of change driven by more versatile equipment has continued to quicken. This has had consequences not only for the way in which news is gathered and distributed, (Beckett, 2008; Shirky, 2008; Tumber and Webster, 2006: 82) but also, potentially, for the content of news reports themselves.

After this first 'live television war' in Iraq in the 1990s, another followed in the next decade. By then, satellite equipment had become even more portable. In Iraq in December 2003, my BBC colleagues and I drove to a village outside Baghdad and, after a brief period setting up cameras and transmission equipment, did a morning's broadcasting about the lives and hopes of the people we met there. The end of Saddam Hussein's regime had changed our relationship with our audience too. The streets emptied as I began my first broadcast. I wondered what had happened. The residents had rushed into the village cafe to see their homes on the BBC – something that had only recently become possible. Under Saddam Hussein, it had been illegal for ordinary citizens to own satellite dishes. Now contributors were also audience members – with implications for our journalism. If our material could be seen in the places from which we were reporting, there might be consequences for us, and for our contributors. A few days later, we were broadcasting live from the place where Saddam Hussein had just been captured – although on that occasion, we were prevented from visiting his hiding place until the embedded reporters, those who had agreed to work with, and under the regulations of, the occupying US forces, had been flown in by helicopter, and given the chance to take the first pictures (I will consider this in greater detail in Chapter 3). If coverage of that conflict was notable for the ever-increasing portability of television equipment, and for the opportunities it afforded non-western international television channels like Al-Jazeera to enhance their reputation (Seib, 2008: 20), it was perhaps more notable for the emergence of the internet as a major influence. Bloggers demonstrated as never before in war that they were a significant force able to both complement, and challenge, the way the established media worked. The 'citizen journalist' arrived in conflict zones alongside the kind of 'civilian journalist' first personified by William Howard Russell – and some of those bloggers were combatants, too. The lines between the roles of civilian, soldier and journalist were becoming less distinct.

In January 2009, Israel sent its forces into the Gaza Strip to try to stop rocket attacks launched from the territory. Perhaps because the Israeli Army knew that its offensive, in such a densely populated place, would probably kill hundreds of civilians, it banned journalists from entering Gaza. Those Palestinian journalists who were inside the territory at the time of Israel's invasion worked hard to fill the information gap (Chapter 6 looks in detail at the reporting of this offensive) – aided by countless volunteers who gathered on their mobile phones material that was broadcast around the world. User-generated content or UGC had arrived in war reporting. That conflict began an ongoing debate about objectivity, and freedom of movement for the media, in the age when countless people carry with them at all times the technology – a simple mobile phone – that enables them to broadcast. It began a debate too about whether Israel's ban on journalists – like that employed by the Sri Lankan Army in their offensive against the Tamil Tigers shortly afterwards – could actually be effective when so many people were able to post material.

Conclusion

I mentioned above the factors – such as access, and the journalist's personal involvement – which I believe are the forces that shape conflict reporting day to day. I also identified politics and technology as the most important wider influences, those which are concerned with more than the reporter's immediate surroundings.

A case could also be made for adding ownership to this list. The example of News Corporation's *Fox News* comes to mind, with its Iraq coverage by such correspondents as the 'hyperpatriotic' Geraldo Rivera (Carruthers, 2011: 249). While ownership undoubtedly affects what appears in the editorial columns, it cannot influence what a reporter – far from the newsroom – actually *sees* on the battlefield. In other words, it does not, and cannot, affect the process of *newsgathering* in anything like the same way as politics and technology. Vincent Mosco has written:

> What we have learned is that the person who sits on top matters less than the application of strict industrial models to media production and strict financial accounting that puts the interests of revenue, profit, and stock value over all other considerations.
>
> (2009: 69)

I think this is especially true of the coverage of conflicts, which is often very expensive, and not obviously in the 'interests of revenue, profit, and stock value'. In Chapter 4, I suggest that news values largely follow the importance that political elites place upon a conflict. I would argue that, in conflict reporting, these political influences represent a more powerful factor than ownership. For that reason, for the purposes of this book, I subsume ownership into my broad definition of politics, above, rather than give it its own category.

So how influential are politics and technology now? One of the most important questions today is whether the model of war reporting which we have had and followed since William Russell – that of the civilian correspondent travelling to war with the aim of describing it – is any longer adequate on its own. At the same time as our international political scene has moved on from the certainties which characterized the second half of the last century – superpowers and their respective camps dominating the world – so our media have moved on from the era where big broadcasters and newspapers were the only outlets with real influence. From the days of William Howard Russell onwards, changing technology has been a major force in the evolution of conflict reporting. As the pace of technological change has quickened over the last twenty years, so has the pace of change in the way in which we as journalists do our jobs. In Georgia in 1992, we needed a large satellite dish even to make an international phone call. In 2008, I could rely on being able to do that from a small hand-held device which also permitted me to send text, photos and video. And that small, hand-held device was not a vastly expensive piece of equipment which only a major news organization could afford – it was something much more widely available. In seeking to predict how that massive change will affect the way forward for war reporting, I will return to my second Russell, James Russell, and his letter from Waterloo. I know this letter because James Russell was my ancestor, and my family still has it.

Where William Howard Russell watched the suffering of the wounded and dying, observing them 'making signals towards our lines', James Russell's words offer us a different perspective: closer perhaps, to that of the men dying from their wounds. My ancestor survived, but not without having undergone great hardship. His is the individual account of one who was so involved in the action he described that his very life was at stake. Until the conventional war correspondent came along, his was the kind of storytelling that people far removed from the action would have to rely upon. It was the story told by a combatant, a non-professional reporter, who had a clear interest in the conflict which he witnessed. That is not to say it is without value as we seek to learn what happened. Like good reporting, his letter demonstrates a clear understanding of the way that the battle unfolded; of the wider strategic significance of the action in which he was involved: 'when night came on the Prussians came up and attacked the French and put them totally to the route [sic],' he writes to his family.

We have now been pursuing them this [sic] 3 days and never have been able to come up with them. We are in hopes that another firm battle will settle this business for we are now two days march into France without interruption and report says his army is almost annihilated.

He begins his letter by telling his family that he is safe ('I am once more in the kind providence of God spared to inform you that I am in good health in the hopes that this will find you and my family enjoying the same rich Blessing'), then goes on, almost with the technique of a filmmaker, to 'pull out' and describe the battle itself. Only towards the end does he return to himself as an individual.

> My Dr [i.e. 'Dear' – JR] I would change the subject and inform you of myself. I have lost all my things. This day I am getting a dead Frenchman's shirt washed to put on. My horse was wounded and sent into Brussels during the action and has lost my whole kit so I am now as I stand.

So in this brief account, whose primary purpose is to communicate with loved ones, we have a despatch from the front line. We learn of the way the battle was fought and won; read speculation of how it might affect the course of the entire war; see a little of the experience of a cavalryman who has had a brush with death, and now has only his enemy's shirt on his back. Of the two Russells, William Howard, and James, my ancestor's account predates his professional and much more widely renowned namesake by some forty years. Now, though, almost two centuries after the Battle of Waterloo, the technology changing every aspect of our lives is also giving new weight to war-zone accounts which are the modern equivalents of my great-great-great-great-grandfather's. His story is told in a handwritten letter which various of his descendants have, at different times, copied in more legible contemporary handwriting; into type; electronically. Now it is easy to imagine the original's modern counterpart as a series of tweets or Facebook updates, distributed to 'followers' and 'friends' and perhaps, via them, onto the liveblog of a major news organization: messages which compete with, and complement, the account of the professional journalist in telling the story of war.

Summary

- the 'two Russells': the letter-writing soldier and the professional war correspondent
- politics and technology: the two factors with the greatest influence on the reporting of conflict
- newspapers, radio, television, live television and the internet all taking their turn as the latest medium
- Vietnam as the first war broadcast on television, Iraq 1991 as the first war on *live* television
- new kinds of conflict in the post-Cold War, post-September 11 world
- non-professional content competes with, and complements, professional content

2 Access

You turn the corner. The street before you is empty – although it is the middle of the working day, and you passed a busy market just a few hundred metres back. Where are all the people? Blocks of flats rise up on either side of the deserted way ahead. You know that somewhere the troops who were advancing towards this area of town must have taken up positions. You suspect that behind the silent windows above your head their enemy is probably trying to work out their next move. All you have to report so far is an empty street. A man in combat clothing, carrying a gun, motions you to stop. You have no story yet, and it looks as if you may not be going any further.

Access is the starting point of all coverage of conflict. It enables the journalist to watch, to listen, to ask the questions that yield the information needed to tell a story. The idea of access must also encompass the reporter's own sense of danger: an understanding of what is an acceptable level of risk. No one – journalist or otherwise – can do their job properly if they are overcome with fear. 'Access' is also dependent on language. In international journalism, every reporter at some time or other, and many most of the time, will have to rely on a third person to translate for them. This barrier to understanding can be just as much of an obstacle to good reporting as the armed man who steps out into the road to block your way. There is a further point here, too. The man blocking the way can block the way out, as well as the way in. The possibility of escape is a key part of the calculation of the risk being taken. If you cannot get out, you may not be able to send your material – although, as with every aspect of journalism, technology is changing the conditions dictating what is, and what is not, possible. Correspondents unable to enter Syria in the spring of 2011 were able to get material from twitter, Facebook and YouTube, in a way that would have been impossible only a few years before. The resulting coverage may have been incomplete, and riddled with caveats, but it was at least coverage.

Since William Howard Russell travelled with British forces to the Crimea, professional journalists have accompanied troops under various conditions in different conflicts. Today, 'embedding' is the name given to the practice of reporters travelling with armies or other armed forces with the latters' knowledge and permission, and under their regulations. The word was first widely used to describe the system developed for journalists travelling with the invading forces in Iraq in 2003, but the practice was not new (Carruthers, 2011: 54; Tumber and Webster, 2006: 20) . Similar systems – although with varying degrees of formality – had operated in Vietnam, and during the Falklands conflict in 1982. Since 2003, the debate around access for journalists in conflict zones has centred on whether or not this is desirable, mutually beneficial or simply a military public relations tactic to ensure favourable coverage.

Studies of journalistic access to conflict

Knightley (1989) writes about the difficulties that William Howard Russell encountered in getting the troops he was accompanying to accept his presence. His experience has been repeated – in various forms – countless times since. Much of the academic literature devoted to considering issues of access, therefore, looks at the relationship between journalists and protagonists, be they civilians or combatants. Morrison and Tumber's *Journalists at War* (1988) concentrates on the Falklands War, but the situations they describe would presumably be recognizable to Russell, and certainly to those working in the period which is my main focus: the 1990s and later. In their study of reporters who sailed to the Falklands with the British Task Force, they write, 'Military priorities were seen as vastly outweighing journalistic needs' (ibid.: 13). While, in a time of proposed defence cuts which mirrors our own, the services were keen to get coverage (ibid.: 23), they also wanted the power to remove reporters should they prove a hindrance (ibid.: 21). It is interesting to read that it was Downing Street, not the Ministry of Defence, which decided to increase the number of journalists permitted to join the Task Force (ibid.: 2). Politicians granted greater access where combatants wanted less – a clear example of politics as a formative influence on combat reporting.

Many studies (Allan and Zelizer, 2004; Tumber and Palmer, 2004; Tumber and Webster, 2006; Robinson *et al.*, 2010; Carruthers, 2011) have examined embedding for the effect that it has on the kind of coverage produced. Tumber and Palmer note the advantage of the system to the military should relations with journalists become strained: 'the looseness of the guidelines gives military commanders who are less sympathetic to journalists the discretion to remove unwanted reporters' (2004: 28). Allan and Zelizer are right to argue that the debate about embedding in Iraq 'was allowed to displace other lines of enquiry and critique' (2004: 6) but, if it did so, it did so because it was the source of the majority of the coverage seen by audiences during the initial invasion and subsequent occupation – and, for all its faults, it was the best chance most journalists had to get a picture of the way the invasion unfolded.

Tumber and Webster (2006) write chapters on 'Danger and Safety' and 'Training and Protection'; Tumber and Palmer (2004) have a chapter 'The Safety of Journalists'. These represent an important addition to factors – such as military pressure, influence and restrictions – more widely considered in the existing literature. But these are not the only, nor probably even the most important, factors in the decision-making process involved when a news organization or an individual journalist embarks on such deployments. Instead, the most important part of the decision-making process is the first of the three questions that will form the basis of my approach in this chapter on access:

1   What will the journalist see?
2   How safe will he or she be?
3   How is changing technology affecting the concept of access?

I will consider questions (1) and (2) at length in this chapter. I will refer to question (3) throughout, but examine it in greater detail in Chapters 5, 6 and 7. Question (1) is obvious. I understand it to mean not just what the reporter will actually witness, but who they will be able to talk to and who they will not. Question (2) might seem surprising to some outsiders, but reporting conflict has become increasingly dangerous in the last two decades, and the situation shows no sign of changing. With some exceptions, like those I mentioned above, this is not considered in enough detail in most academic accounts of conflict reporting. For aside from the issue of protecting oneself from harm, risking death or injury also means risking professional failure by not being able to despatch your report.

What will we see? 'Embeds' and 'unilaterals'; 'open' and 'controlled' reporting

In television news, 'What will we see?' is often the first question the desk editor asks the reporter on assignment. If access in television terms means pictures, for other platforms it can mean audio or simply text. In any case, the reporter needs the chance to witness events at first hand, and to describe them – what Allan and Zelizer call 'being there' (2004: 5). If embedding is going to help them to do that, a reporter is likely to accept it, for all its drawbacks. The journalist's overriding concern is to get his or her material to their audience. Failure to do that within the deadline – whatever the reason – is total failure. An assignment that satisfied all questions of journalistic ethics and safety might be laudable indeed. If, for all that, it failed to produce a report, it would be worthless. That is why access – 'being there' – is so important, even if it has limitations. Robinson *et al.* summarize the effects that they feel these limitations had in coverage of the 2003 invasion of Iraq: 'the story was all about winning and losing, rather than offering a consideration of the context in which the war was fought' (2010: 84). Such shortcomings are legitimate concerns, but they do not override the fact that journalists accept embeds because they are either the best, or perhaps the least bad, way of seeing a key part of the whole story. A news report is brief, and compiled at speed. Complete context and balance can often only be provided over time. Embedding may also be chosen for another reason, inadequately reflected in academic studies. If journalists accompany troops on operations, they acquire a degree of knowledge they can use to reject any claims from armies that they do not know what they are talking about – a tactic frequently engaged to try to discredit unfavourable coverage. As Tumber and Webster say of the 2003 invasion of Iraq,

> It was the military and the government that agreed to the embedding of journalists and a few days following when the coverage was not going exactly how they wanted or intended, media organisations were accused of not providing explanations about the bigger picture.
> (2006: 25)

Military and civilian authorities are often too eager to accuse the media of inaccuracy when things start going wrong: having been there strengthens the rebuttal of such criticism.

The access afforded by embedding does not blind correspondents to the system's potential pitfalls and shortcomings. The BBC's Ben Brown writes about his experience travelling with British troops entering the southern Iraqi city of Basra in 2003, 'Reporters are supposed to be observers of the battlefield, not participants. I wondered if, by being so close to the British troops, I had somehow crossed an invisible line' (2003: 32). 'Embeds' are often compared with 'unilaterals', journalists who make their own way in the war zone. If they meet troops, it may be by chance just as much as by design. In many cases, this kind of reporting offers the opportunity to gather rare and exclusive pictures. It is also seen, sometimes, as more dangerous. Advancing troops may well fire on vehicles or people which they do not immediately recognize as friendly. The most infamous recent such case is the 2003 death of ITN reporter Terry Lloyd. His translator, Hussein Osman, was also killed, and the cameraman, Fred Nerac, is missing, believed dead. The most widely credited version of events suggests that US marines shot at them, but no one has ever been charged or convicted (BBC News, 2008b).

Rather than looking at journalists as 'embeds' or 'unilaterals', I prefer to define not the reporters themselves, but the kind of reporting they are able to contribute. In practice, most reporters who have covered conflict have done so with armies, with irregular fighters and on their own. There are exceptions: journalists working for military publications who have no desire to go anywhere other than with the troops and, at the other end of the spectrum, journalists who feel it is wrong to travel with an army. Most fall somewhere in between. Therefore, rather than talking of the kind of reporter, I prefer to think in terms of the kind of reporting. I divide this into two broad categories, which I call 'open' and 'controlled'.

Chechnya 1994 and 2000: two conflicts, and two kinds of reporting

At the end of 1994, the Russian government sent troops to Chechnya, a region in the south of the Russian Federation whose separatist leadership had in effect taken it out of Moscow's control. The Russian government was determined to reverse that scenario. Some eighteen months later, in the summer of 1996, a truce was brokered. There was no clear victor, and tens of thousands of civilians were among those killed. The conflict became known as the first Chechen war. The autumn of 1999 saw a series of bombings of apartment blocks in Russia. Hundreds of people died. The bombers struck during the night when many residents were asleep. The Russian government, under the leadership of the then prime minister, Vladimir Putin, blamed Chechen separatists. Moscow launched a massive new military offensive to punish and destroy those they held responsible. This became known as the second Chechen war.

I covered both conflicts. Even in the relatively short space of time between the start of the first, and the end of the second,[3] the way in which reporters worked had changed dramatically. The first was a clear example of 'open' access reporting; the second of 'controlled'. In the first case, the only real limit put on a reporter's movements was their own sense of safety, and the degree of risk they were willing to accept. There was no one, either from the Russian Army, or the Chechen fighters, who formally decided the areas in which journalists could and could not work. In the second case, the Russian military imposed strict controls on reporters, in effect banning them from entering the region of Chechnya at all. Only later, once the conflict had to a large degree subsided, although not ended, did the Russian Army begin to organize visits to Chechnya for journalists. 'Organize' is the important word here. Having decided that allowing journalists to travel where they wanted in the first war had resulted in some unfavourable coverage, and having realized that banning them altogether was time-consuming and, ultimately, unworkable, the authorities settled for granting access – but only on their terms. Again, as in Vietnam and the Falklands, this was a kind of embed – three years before the invasion of Iraq when the practice became so widespread.

On those trips, we reporters were completely dependent on the Russian authorities, the military in particular, for almost everything. The daily schedule of travel and visits was set by them, and the pace was sometimes frustratingly slow. Including travel time to and from Moscow, I spent a week just getting enough material for two television reports of a kind that could normally be made in a day or less. All transport from the garrison town of Mozdok in North Ossetia onwards was arranged by the Russian Army, which was naturally responsible for security too. We were accompanied everywhere by a Russian official who spoke Chechen – very rare for Slavic Russians – which led me to suspect that he was probably a former, or current, intelligence agent. Although this was a trip for foreign journalists, it was also attended by a woman claiming to be a correspondent from a Russian interior ministry publication. She spoke excellent English. Anyone of her age – she was then around fifty – who had learned English to such a high standard had most likely done so with the approval and encouragement of the Soviet authorities. Her role seemed to be that of propagandist for the Russian official position. When we failed to do so, she would ask questions of those to whom we were introduced in a manner which assumed sympathy with the Russian authorities' version of events.

The two types of access – open and controlled – produced completely different stories. In the first war, with no limits placed on our activities except those dictated by a sense of danger, we were able to talk to a much greater number of people. As always in any war zone, any single day's reporting is by its nature limited in its scope, but on those days we were able to gather a much wider range of voices – so our coverage gave a truer picture of the overall situation. In a single day, it was possible to talk to Russian troops – at checkpoints on the approaches to Grozny; civilians within the city; the Chechen fighters who moved among them. These differing viewpoints were not available to reporters who were confined to one side or another. In particular, our access illuminated one murderously clumsy side of the Russian military's ham-fisted tactics. Many of the civilians we encountered sheltering in the cellars beneath their blocks of flats were actually ethnic Russians: no more Chechen than the soldiers who were flattening the city. In Soviet times, many Russians had chosen to make Grozny their home – not least because the climate was so much milder than most of the rest of the vast territory over which Moscow ruled. Where the Chechen population of Grozny had in many cases been able to leave the city to stay with relatives in outlying villages, the Russians were trapped – shivering in fear of the fury of the state they had long relied upon to protect them. From a reporter's point of view, their stories represented a strong human-interest angle on the bombardment, and an indictment of Moscow's myopic military planning. It was bombing its own people more than it was the targets it dubbed 'bandits' and 'terrorists'.

In the second war, with our military escort, and minders from the Russian Federal Security Service (FSB – the main successor agency to the KGB), we were taken by bus to see the villages of northern Chechnya, which, as the official Russian account of the war had it, had been 'liberated' from the 'terrorists'. At the time, the area over which the Russian government had control was growing southwards – towards the Caucasus Mountains where the rebel fighters had their strongholds. The places we were taken had been chosen to show that life was slowly returning to normal. Outwardly, during the day, in the presence of Russian troops, that seemed to be the case – if the presence of Russian troops did not disqualify this from being normal. What we could not do on that occasion was talk to people. At least one of our interviewees – a woman who told us of the number of civilians who had been killed by the rebels – was coached by our guide as she spoke. Others shied away from saying anything at all. The material we gathered was little more than an illustration of the Russian official version of events – one which was woefully incomplete. We were deprived of the opportunity even to use 'the familiar practice of juxtaposing every "he said" with a "she said"' (Carruthers, 2011: 230). This was an example of the worst kind of 'controlled' reporting – an exercise that is largely a waste of the time of everyone involved. We did not get the kind of material necessary to help us to tell a story; if we weren't going to use it, our guides had largely made the journey in vain, too. It is in 'controlled' cases like these that the reporter – if they have to use the material because they have nothing else – is often obliged to write about the restrictions under which they were working. 'The Russian authorities do not permit journalists to travel freely in Chechnya' and similar phrases often appeared at the beginning of scripts.

In addition to the restrictions placed upon reporters by the Russian authorities, coverage was also shaped by the political situation, and the technology at the disposal both of the reporters, and the Russian military. The second war was fought at the beginning of Vladimir Putin's tenure at the top of Russian public life, and he was very publicly identified with the renewed military campaign. The greater controls placed upon the news media seemed to mirror what Mr Putin then called the 'dictatorship of the law'. Unlike in the first war, reporters had smaller, more portable satellite telephones, enabling them to send voice reports, text and still pictures during brief visits to the bombed-out city centre of Grozny. In both cases, Morrison and Tumber's verdict on the Falklands War – 'Military priorities were seen as vastly outweighing journalistic needs' (1988: 13) – was applicable, albeit in different senses. In the first war, the Russian Army was too preoccupied with its enemy to bother about reporters; in the second, it did its best to make sure reporters' requirements were subservient to military priorities.

Southern Iraq and Stalingrad, a critical assessment of two different 'embeds': Evan Wright's *Generation Kill* and Vassily Grossman's *A Writer at War*

Generation Kill (2009) is Evan Wright's account of his 'embed' with a unit of US marines during the invasion of Iraq. Part of his book is also about what Wright comes to understand about himself, especially when the unit comes under attack. His reflections open a door through which we glimpse something of his life away from Iraq, perhaps offering an insight into the kind of person who can successfully function as a reporter of conflict.

But in my first experience at being in the midst of heavy gunfire – from machine guns to mortars to Marine artillery still slamming into the city over our heads – I feel surprisingly calm. While the Marines might possess that 'adolescent sense of invulnerability,' I have the more adult handicap of having always lived in denial. It's a problem for which I've attended therapy sessions and self-help groups in an effort to overcome, originally at the urging of a now ex-wife. But I find that in a pitched fire-fight, denial serves one very well. I simply refuse to believe anyone's going to shoot me.

That is not to say I'm not scared. In fact, I'm so scared I feel not completely in my body.

(2009: 133)

He also addresses the issue of agreeing to give up communication – in this case, as in others, a condition of embedding.

Initially, the battalion had planned for me to spend the invasion riding with the support company in the rear. But in exchange for handing over my satellite phone – severing all contact with the outside world – First Recon's commander, Lieutenant Colonel Ferrando, allows me to move in with Second Bravo Platoon.

(ibid.: 36)

The agreement puts him at the heart of the action as the invasion begins – and it succinctly sums up the choice which every correspondent has to consider when offered the opportunity to travel with an army. The interests of reporters and army public relations officials can coincide – Carruthers describes such an arrangement as a 'cosying-up that promises certain benefits to all parties' (2011: 54) – especially when the media organization the journalist is working for is broadly supportive of the action in which the military is engaged. More often, these interests do not coincide. What follows is an uneasy game. Each participant closely watches the other, not wanting to lose. Defeat for the journalist comes with the feeling that that he or she is willingly submitting to censorship, probably against their own interests and better judgement. For military personnel, it lies in the worry that, rather than gaining positive publicity, they are voluntarily compromising their own security, or allowing themselves to be portrayed in a bad light.

Having surrendered his satellite phone, Wright, who was writing for *Rolling Stone* magazine, meets some of the soldiers he will accompany as they invade Iraq. They are wary of him, and of his intentions. His first meeting with one of the marines is unpleasantly tense.

'So you came here for a war, huh? You like war?' He continues to squeeze my hand, then puts his face about eight inches from mine and stares with unblinking, electric-blue eyes. His smile begins to twitch. 'I hope you have fun in this war, reporter.'

(2009: 37)

Generation Kill conveys the complete isolation that comes with a lengthy 'embed' such as this. Wright refers (ibid.: 89) to the news that the marines are sometimes able to receive on short-wave radio. It seems to be more useful than anything they receive through military channels. There is a point here about technology, too. Then the US Army in Iraq could expect Evan Wright to give up his satellite phone for weeks at a time, but for how much longer will that be the case? In the age of the ready access to social networking sites and ever-increasing mobile-phone coverage, when the use of Twitter is challenging legal rulings on reporting,[4] this kind of isolation may not be possible much longer. This is good for the reporter who wants to stay in touch, but perhaps bad for the reporter who wants to be trusted with information which might once have been off the record. That which may be instantly tweeted may remain unsaid. All reporters have experienced a source ending a quiet or whispered – and extremely informative – conversation when a third person approaches. There may now be an increasing number of circumstances in which those conversations will not even begin.

Generation Kill is a close-up view of troops in modern war. It is extremely illuminating on the nature of the marines and their daily lives; less so on the bigger picture. That is not Wright's purpose, but, by showing in such detail part of that bigger picture, he increases our understanding of it. The effect is that we feel embedded ourselves. The occasional references to the BBC as the only, one-way contact with the outside world serve strongly to reinforce this sense of being cut off. Wright's task as a reporter is to overcome the distance that separates him from his reader – who will almost certainly never have experienced events similar to the ones that Wright describes. So when we consider the purpose, the impact of such assignments, it is important to understand, as not all academic observers seem to, that the journalist's purpose is what Allan and Zelizer call 'being there' (2004: 5), 'rather than offering a consideration of the context in which the war was fought.' (Robinson *et al.*, 2010: 84). Context is indispensable, but the 'embed' is not always best placed to provide it, and so should not necessarily be expected to do so. Reporters know this. As Tumber and Webster write, some reporters make a judgement that sets 'against *de facto* censorship the access that being an embed allowed' (2006: 168).

This sense of isolation is also present in Vassily Grossman's *A Writer at War* (2006). Grossman would not have recognized the word, but today he too would be called an 'embed'. His reporting was little known outside the former Soviet Union before 2005, when extracts from his notebooks, edited and translated by Antony Beevor and Luba Vinogradova, were published in English. I include Grossman here for what he tells us about the experience of an 'embed' in a different war. Grossman is a rare talent, the star of his generation, called upon to shine when his country faced destruction in the Second World War. He reported on the Red Army's experience of its war against the Nazis: from Hitler's invasion of the western Soviet Union in June 1941, through the battle of Stalingrad, the liberation of the death camp at Treblinka, to victory in Berlin. As a war reporter, a chronicler of all the horrors of this conflict, Grossman is without equal. He shared the dangers and the hardships of the troops whose campaigns he so carefully covered. At the outset of the war, like so many reporters before him and since, he faces a struggle even to get where he is going.

> There were black holes and craters from bombs everywhere along the railway. One could see trees broken by explosions. In the fields there were thousands of peasants, men and women, digging anti-tank ditches.
>
> We watch the sky nervously and decided to jump off the train if the worst came to the worst. It was moving quite slowly. The moment we arrived in Novozybkov there was an air raid. A bomb fell by the station forecourt. This train wasn't going any further.
>
> (2006: 8)

In a few spare sentences, Grossman gives us a complete picture of the Soviet Union, already battered by aerial bombardment, preparing to resist invasion. The image of thousands of people digging ditches anticipates the colossal struggle which lies ahead. Then we are snapped out of this contemplation by a bomb landing near the station and forcing him to seek another way forward. The urgency, unpredictability and extreme danger of his situation are all forcefully impressed upon us.

Grossman's fate was to be assigned to epic historical events, and his reporting is equal to it. His access is good. As the war goes on, his fame increases, and that improves his opportunities still further. During the battle of Stalingrad, at great personal risk – danger was not something that Grossman allowed to limit his reporting – he interviews a sniper from his position overlooking German lines. It is a long interview, in which Grossman just lets the man tell his story. The sniper, Anatoly Chekhov, is aged barely twenty, but already brutalized by the war in which he has spent his youth.

> When I first got the rifle, I couldn't bring myself to kill a living being: one German was standing there for about four minutes, talking, and I let him go. When I killed my first one, he fell at once. Another one ran out and stooped over the killed one, and I knocked him down too ... when I first killed, I̦ was shaking all over: the man was only walking to get some water! ... I felt scared: I'd killed a person! Then I remembered our people and started killing them without mercy.
>
> (ibid.: 157)

With a dedication similar to that of the sniper, Grossman carefully listens to his subject and records his words and feelings. The result of his extraordinary access, the reward for his risk-taking, is a stunning piece of combat reportage.

How safe will we be?

Grossman does not write at length about any fear for his own safety. He seems completely drawn into his country's fight for its survival. But the safety of reporters covering conflict has become such an issue that Tumber and Palmer have gone so far as to suggest, writing of the 2003 invasion of Iraq, 'The high death toll has led to concerns that Gulf War II could spell the end of the independent witnessing of war' (2004: 36). While the number of reporters who travelled to Libya in the spring of 2011 shows that there is still no shortage of volunteers, the deaths there of Tim Hetherington and Chris Hondros showed that the risks were real, even for such experienced journalists. Journalists covering war have always accepted that what they do is dangerous. It is only relatively recently that they have had to accept that the chance of someone deliberately trying to kill them has greatly increased. The International Federation of Journalists entitled its report on journalists and media staff killed in 2009 *The End of a Deadly Decade*, noting that 'the adoption of resolution 1738 by the United Nations Security Council in 2006, which called for the protection of journalists in conflict zones and for proper investigation into violent attacks on media, has largely been ignored' (2009: 2). The IFJ's figures are backed up by those of Reporters without Borders (2011) and the Committee to Protect Journalists (2011). Many of those deaths which led the IFJ to label the first ten years of this century 'a deadly decade' were deaths of individuals killed by criminals or murderous politicians (or some characters who are at home in both categories) in order to silence them. Others were killed simply because armies felt like firing on them: notorious examples include Taras Protsyuk and Jose Couso, killed by American shells at the Palestine Hotel in Baghdad in April 2003, or James Miller gunned down by the Israeli Army in southern Gaza the same year. The job of reporting conflict is becoming more and more dangerous, and, despite the fine words and worthy ideals of UN resolution 1738, governments have a poor record of actually doing anything about it.

The reporter working in 'controlled' conditions is largely forced to surrender responsibility for his or her safety – whether that is a good thing or not depends upon the nature of the assignment, and the nature of the combatants the journalist is travelling with. I will conclude this chapter with an account of my assignment with the Israeli Army in Gaza in 2003, analysing it as a case study of the points about access and security to which I have already referred.

Case study 1: accompanying Israeli troops in an attack on Gaza

On the evening of 5 March 2003, two weeks before the United States and its allies began their invasion of Iraq, I received a telephone call from the Israeli Army's Southern Command. They asked me if I wanted to go on an operation that night. My contact, whom I knew from a meeting he had previously arranged for me with a senior officer in the Southern Command, forbade me from telling anyone where I was going. Another officer from the army press service called shortly after-wards to stress their demand for secrecy. I was given very little detail, only told to be at the crossing point between the Gaza Strip and Israel a little later that evening. The decision to go was not a difficult one. I knew that this was a rare opportunity. As it turned out, this was the only time that I was offered this kind of access in the whole of my two years in Gaza. I also knew that the opportunity to cover even one story from a particular side gives you an insight that can inform your reporting for weeks or even months to come. I had already been in Gaza for more than six months, and reported extensively on the effect the conflict[5] had had on the territory and its people. In so doing, I had always striven to reflect Israel's point of view – with a very limited knowledge of how its troops actually operated. So the journalistic reasons for accepting the offer were clear. There was another, ethical dimension which I think might have led some reporters to turn the request down. In many of Israel's military raids into Gaza, their troops killed civilians. They almost certainly would tonight. That being so, was I right to accompany them? By being with them as a witness, was I accepting that what they were doing was right? Was I risking compromising journalistic ethics in return for access? I considered these questions at the time, although briefly, and not just because time was short. From the point of view of access to information, this was a rare and important chance which I had to take. The best reporting combines experience of as many sides of the story as possible. In Gaza, I spoke to the bereaved and the homeless almost every day. I rarely had the chance to speak to the soldiers who caused the death and destruction.

Personal security is usually a further consideration when deciding whether or not to accept an offer to accompany an army on an operation. On this occasion, that was less of a concern, for two reasons. First, as is usually the case, an army will try to ensure the safety of a reporter, not least because its own reputation might suffer if a civilian under its protection were to come to harm. Second, I knew that the Israelis so vastly outgunned the Palestinian fighters that there was little real prospect of my finding myself in harm's way.

I was to be completely cut off from communication for as long as the operation lasted. It was not the isolation to which Evan Wright was forced to agree, but I was not allowed to use my mobile phone for the duration of the raid. I spoke to the senior producer in Jerusalem to let him know that the armoured column in which I was to travel was about to set off. I knew by then, although I was unable to tell him, that the target of the raid was to be the Jabalya refugee camp, a sprawling and densely populated shanty town at the northern edge of Gaza City. It was inconceivable that there would not be deaths in the coming confrontation.

The column moved off around midnight. I was in an armoured personnel carrier together with a BBC cameraman – an Israeli colleague – and a number of soldiers. The access we got that night was rare, but, in other ways, not especially illuminating. Our understanding of what was happening was restricted to what we could hear going on outside the shell of the armoured personnel carrier, and to what we could see through the turret above our heads. From my knowledge of the geography of the northern Gaza Strip and its roads, I guessed at some point we must have travelled along part of the route that my Palestinian colleague and I had followed as he drove me to the crossing point earlier that evening. At one stage, the column stopped in the middle of Jabalya. It came under fire, although the vehicle in which I was travelling was not hit. Some of the troops left to seek out a suspected militant, but said it was too dangerous for us to go with them. At that point, we did have a view of the street through the open door – but it was the middle of the night, and the only illumination was dim street lighting and tracer fire.

Most of the time our view of what was happening was literally blinkered – limited to the circular hole of the turret above our heads. So while the access afforded by the opportunity to travel with the troops was rare, it was also restricted. For a journalist involved in documenting the Israeli–Palestinian conflict over an extended period, it was invaluable. I was able to put a face to some of the troops who so frequently carried out military operations in the area in which I lived, and from which I reported. I gained an insight – however brief – into the way they carried out those operations. For a reporter covering the story of the night, though, the access I received left many questions unanswered. In this respect, my experience confirmed the criticism of embedding as offering only an incomplete impression (Robinson *et al.*, 2010: 34).

To conclude the account of what happened that night, I reproduce the following extract from my diary, written a few days later.

> Dawn was breaking. The cameraman translated snatches of what he heard on the radio: tank shell fired at man with rpg [rocket-propelled grenade – JR] ... armed man surrounded by kids, sniper needed to shoot him ... house of Hamas man blown up ... explosive device activated from furniture shop.
>
> This last information would prove to be the controversy of the night.
>
> There was a brief delay on the way back. Something which looked like a booby trap was spotted on the route ahead, so we had to wait while it was checked. Sunlight was now coming in the open roof. Occasional bursts of gunfire still rang out.
>
> We arrived back at the assembly point just after 8.30.
>
> Shortly after 9, we were on our way to Jerusalem. On the way, I spoke to the bureau. The incursion was lead story on domestic and

international outlets. Eight people had been killed in the explosion at the furniture shop. Eyewitnesses said it was caused by a shell from a departing tank. It had fired on a crowd which had gathered to watch fire fighters tackling a blaze in the shop, the Palestinians said. Not so, said the Israelis. The explosives had been in the shop, and had been set off by the fire. I had seen nothing, of course, but the agency pictures I saw in the bureau later showed the blast. My untrained eye didn't help me to decide.

As so frequently in the Israeli–Palestinian conflict, the two sides never agreed on what had actually happened. Despite my proximity to the explosion – it could have been one of several which I heard that night – I had no idea of its cause. In this case, my 'good access' actually hampered my reporting of the day's news because my view was so restricted. Note, too, the importance here of language as mentioned at the outset of this chapter. I was relying on a non-professional translation of a radio message which was barely audible above the noise of the battle. Journalists rarely admit the existence of the barrier that language frequently presents, but it can be hugely significant in their understanding of what is happening around them. I can speak Russian. When travelling with the Russian Army in the Caucasus, I knew what they were talking about, whether or not they wanted me to. That made me more aware of my lack of understanding here, where I was forced to rely on someone else's interpretation of what they heard.

To conclude the issue of embedding, I would say that Tumber and Webster's finding from their research, 'Some reporters made a judgement that set against *de facto* censorship the access that being an embed allowed' (2006: 168) rings true. There are drawbacks, of course, and Carruthers is right too to suggest that part of the purpose of the system is to encourage journalists to 'replicate their minders' point of view' (2011: 229). Why else would the Israeli Army have offered the only international reporter who covered the Israeli–Palestinian conflict from Gaza such rare access?

Conclusion: why access for journalists matters

I wrote above that governments have a poor record of protecting journalists. They might do well to pay more attention. One of the most important points about journalists' access is that it can exceed that granted to anyone else. The reporter sometimes has a unique perspective on a conflict – the view of someone permitted to stand on both sides of a fence over which neighbours are warring, and, in passing from one side to the other, able to look down from an upper level onto the battle below. Sometimes, this ability leads to journalists being suspected of espionage, with the attendant peril that involves. At others, it permits them an understanding of a situation which surpasses that of princes and policy-makers. For me, that was especially true of my experience in Gaza, and in South Ossetia. In Gaza, I understood that talk of a peace process (at that time, it was the 'road map' of 2003) was largely meaningless while the ordinary people on each side were becoming further alienated. Once Israel banned Palestinian workers from leaving Gaza to work in Israel (for fear that suicide bombers would come with them), an important relationship ended. Some people on both sides spoke of being cut off from friends. These sentiments were perhaps exaggerated, but the absence of daily personal contact did have an effect. In the two years I was in Gaza, I saw this separation becoming more deeply entrenched, a process that has only continued in the intervening years to the extent that it is now hard to see a way back.

I first visited South Ossetia in October 2006, when the breakaway region of Georgia, which had in effect been outside the control of the Georgian government since 1992, was holding a referendum on independence. I spent a week in Georgia: half in South Ossetia, and half in Tbilisi and elsewhere, reporting on the Georgian Army's desire to join NATO. I learnt that the Georgians and the South Ossetians – already separated for more than fifteen years – were dangerously ignorant of each other's views. The Georgian government officials somehow believed that, if they could make the rest of the country prosperous, South Ossetia would forget the fighting of 1992, and happily return to the fold. They had no idea how wrong they were, how deeply opposed the people of South Ossetia were to such a move. Less than two years later, Georgia was at war with Russia, which supported the separatists, over the territory. Had the Georgian authorities chosen to follow some of the reports filed on the referendum, they might have developed a greater understanding of what they were up against. Instead, they concentrated on trying to portray those of us who were there as ill informed and biased. The most frequent accusation made against any reporter in a conflict zone is a lack of objectivity – the subject of the next chapter.

Summary

- access as the starting point of all conflict reporting: key factors include ability to witness, safety and technology
- a reporter's priority to get the story with embedding, for all its shortcomings, often the best way to do so
- 'open' and 'controlled' reporting; travelling with or without combatants
- journalists as targets: unprecedented number of deaths
- the limits on understanding the full story which can come with accompanying an army
- two 'embeds' from different wars: Evan Wright and Vassily Grossman
- journalists' rare perspective of a conflict from both sides

3 Objectivity

> My fellow journalists called themselves correspondents; I preferred the title of reporter. I wrote what I saw. I took no action. Even an opinion is a kind of action.
>
> (Thomas Fowler, narrator of Graham Greene's *The Quiet American*, 2001)

A loud explosion wakes a reporter. The sound of gunfire follows. The clock says 2.25 am. The reporter lies still for a few moments, trying to work out what is happening in the town around her. Her phone rings. A source who has always been reliable says that troops who had been expected to attack the town are now doing so, and that several civilians have already been killed in the advance. The reporter thanks the source, and begins to sketch out a story that will form the basis of a report for radio, television and the web. There is another explosion – this one so powerful that the windows rattle. A minute or so later, the sound of ambulance sirens breaks a brief silence. The phone rings again. It is the reporter's newsdesk in London. Slightly exasperated, the reporter explains that yes, she's aware of the reports and is trying to check them. She calls a contact from the opposing forces, the ones that appear to be invading the town where she had, until a short time ago, been sleeping. They have nothing to say, except to confirm, off the record, that an operation against 'terrorist infrastructure' is underway. It is 2.45 am. The newsdesk calls again, asking if the first news report will be ready by 3 am. In this war, the troops that are attacking enjoy massive military superiority. They are better trained and equipped. They have also been regularly accused by human rights groups of needlessly causing civilian casualties, although these allegations have not always proved true. It is 2.50 am. The reporter dials in to London and sends a forty-second radio report which is published on the internet and aired on television and radio at 3 am. At 3.15 am, the spokesman for the invading army is on the phone to the reporter's news organization – furious that 'unsubstantiated rumours' have been published. The spokesman warns that he is convinced that the news organization has sent a reporter to the town because they want to report 'terrorist propaganda', and advises that the reporter's future accreditation to work in the territory controlled by the troops is under threat.

The idea of objectivity is central to all journalism: whether the reporter strives to adhere to it, or knowingly rejects it. There are occasions, even in journalistic cultures where objectivity is usually highly prized, when the latter is the case. Those occasions are almost always in time of war. As Silvio Waisbord observes of the US media after September 11, 'The "journalism of crisis" was a journalism that snubbed the professional requirements of detachment and objectivity and willingly embraced patriotic partisanship' (2002: 206). Whatever the circumstances, objectivity is a concept that lies at the heart of all editorial decision-making. This is as true of the fictional reporter above as she put together her first story as it is of the editor in London who decided that the story should become the lead. When the story in question is one of war, the question of objectivity is especially pressing – misleading or incomplete information can not only put the reporter in danger, it can cause a conflict to escalate. In the worst case, it becomes a matter of life and death.

Objectivity and impartiality

Objectivity in conflict journalism involves the correspondent striving to keep his or her own political and religious views, cultural prejudices, professional allegiances and financial interests, from influencing their reporting. It also includes the idea of impartiality, which is generally taken to mean the quality of giving equal weight to differing accounts, provided that their probable reliability or otherwise is adequately reflected.

Any discussion of objectivity has to determine the effect that the idea has on the information communicated to an audience; the way it influences reporting. A journalist goes to a conflict zone to find information, and send it on. The task is not to strive towards some ideal goal of objectivity, or have one's prose die a heroic metaphorical death in the process. The task is to tell a story – and objectivity is a means to that end, not an end in itself. Morrison and Tumber's notion of 'objectivity not as a state, but as a procedure' (1988: 127) is a useful description.

Studies of the idea of objectivity in conflict reporting

Objectivity in conflict reporting is the subject of a complex and continuing debate. For reasons of simplicity and space, I have limited my review to a few works which I feel make especially relevant and enduring contributions to that debate. Morrison and Tumber (1988) and Tumber and Prentoulis (2003) fall into this category. Tumber and Prentoulis write

> As the major signifier associated with the occupation of journalism, 'objectivity' is associated and often confused with ideas of 'truth', 'impartiality', 'balance' and 'neutrality'. For example, a journalist's aim may be to reach the truth (and in order to approach the truth they may need to be impartial) but that does not necessarily imply that the means used or the means that could be used, are objective.
>
> (2003: 215–16)

This seems to build on Morrison and Tumber's idea of objectivity as a procedure, referred to above, and makes an important point about the way in which objectivity is indeed confused with impartiality, which is why I felt it necessary to separate them earlier in this chapter. However, I would argue that Morrison and Tumber's idea of objectivity as a procedure becomes too narrowly defined when they develop it further. 'To be objective does not mean to be accurate in some ultimate sense, but to follow the accepted procedures of the journalistic community' (1988: 127). To journalists, objectivity may be a 'procedure', although they might be more likely to think of it also as a value. 'The accepted procedures of the journalistic community' almost suggests unthinking obedience to a professional code. As a reporter, I was never motivated by the idea that 'we do it this way because that's the rule'. Objectivity was a guiding principle – something followed because it had a worth – not something that was accepted without question. Bell's discussion of the journalism of *attachment* (see Chapter 2) and, I hope, my writing this book, shows that journalists themselves are willing to discuss the concept of objectivity. The phrase 'accepted procedures' implies an absence of such discussion. Carruthers (2011) uses a similar expression when she writes of 'professional norms of objectivity and balance that appear to institutionalize, rather than eliminate, certain forms of bias' (2011: 43). While the example she gives (ibid.: 42) of Judith Miller has become notorious, would it be fair to suggest that such reporting is the norm? It depends on what kind of journalism is being considered.

Certainly, as a foreign correspondent, I was sometimes surprised by the willingness of my colleagues covering British politics to accept what the spin doctors told them. Carruthers rightly notes that such reporters are 'dependent on elite approval for access to the corridors of power' (ibid.: 43). Those who cover conflict usually do so far from the corridors of power, and so are less subject to such pressures. Anna Politkovskaya, the Russian journalist famous for her reporting of conflict and human rights abuses in the North Caucasus, and whose work I discuss later in this chapter, was an outstanding example of a refusal to seek 'elite approval' – even when that refusal probably got her killed.

Issues of objectivity from professional experience

I want to look in detail at two broad categories which, I feel from my own experience, include most of the ideas of objectivity usually discussed in newsrooms and in the field.

First, there is the reporter's own attempt to cover conflict in an objective manner following their own assessments of the situations in which they find themselves, and the information that they are able to gather from those situations. Second, there is the question of if and how they manage to do that as they listen to accounts from people involved in the conflict, either as combatants or non-combatants, and those who are not directly involved, but who are striving to present and promote the cause of one side or the other. The role of public relations agencies in recent conflicts, especially the war between Russia and Georgia in 2008, gives this consideration added importance. I will look at that issue in detail in the next chapter.

On my second night in Gaza – I had not yet formally taken up my post as BBC correspondent but I was there to meet my future colleagues in the BBC Arabic Service, and find accommodation – the Israeli Army attacked and destroyed a factory on the eastern edge of Gaza City. The Israelis said that the factory was being used to manufacture mortars. They came into Gaza under cover of darkness, set explosives and blasted the place apart. No one was killed, despite an exchange of fire between the soldiers and Palestinian fighters. The next morning, I accompanied my colleague from the BBC Arabic Service, Fayed Abushammala, to the scene.

A crowd had gathered to gawp and shake their heads, but there was not much to see. There was no sign of smoke or fire. The factory looked like it had not been much to begin with. Now it was nothing. The metal frame of what had once been the walls and the roof stood alone against the sky. Sheets of corrugated iron which had completed the structure lay scattered around. In the centre, which had presumably been the shop floor, lay piles of twisted metal and parts of machines. Whatever the factory had really been making, it wouldn't be making it any longer. We met one of the owners. I gathered that the factory had cut stone and marble. It had a special bench for the purpose. This equipment was also to be found in Israel, but having the work done there, according to the man from the factory, cost twice as much. He said that the factory had been destroyed because the Israeli Army wanted to wreck his business and provide more trade for Israeli stonecutters. He showed us a brochure advertising the machine that he said had been destroyed. In the wreckage, you could just recognize machine parts shown in the glossy pictures. He also pointed to a huge wheel, part of the mechanism, which had apparently been thrown forward from its normal place. The explosion had been one of great force.

Who was telling the truth? I reflected then that this was the challenge I would now face every day as I continued my assignment – rummaging through the rubble of conflicting accounts in the hope of finding what I was looking for. Had they been making mortars at the factory? They might have been. There certainly were factories in Gaza City that were, so why not this one? It would have been easy enough to remove any obvious signs of mortar manufacture in the immediate aftermath, before the curious arrived. In an incident some months later, Palestinian journalists were beaten when they arrived at the scene of an explosion too soon for their own good. They had happened on the aftermath of a 'work accident', as the Israeli Army euphemistically referred to a blast which they suspected had been caused by careless bomb-makers. The hapless reporters had arrived before the bomb factory had had time to clear away what they did not want others to see. Here, the factory owner's claim that he had been targeted for commercial reasons seemed hard to believe. The Israelis would surely have been unlikely to launch a mission so apparently sophisticated to punish a factory which was undercutting the prices charged by Israeli businesses.

My thoughts were not forensic analysis, though. They were speculation. And although I was used to having to try to work out who was telling the truth, arriving in Gaza meant I was starting afresh. I had no experience of previous attacks like this to draw on. This would have been an easy enough story to write. By the standards of the region it was a pretty minor incident. Arriving on a similarly confusing scene with dead bodies and screaming relatives among the wreckage would be a far greater challenge.

There is a broader point to be made here too. I said in my definition of objectivity above that part of it was 'giving equal weight to differing accounts, provided that their probable reliability or otherwise is adequately reflected'. This poses a further question about the principle of objectivity. A reporter such as I was when I witnessed the aftermath of the Israeli raid on my second day in Gaza could be said to be completely objective because he or she might arrive upon the scene with no prior knowledge of what had happened, and simply relay what he or she found. I would argue that that is not necessarily objectivity so much as ignorance. As time went on, and I witnessed such scenes more frequently, I became far more astute at guessing where the truth might lie – in other words, better at 'adequately reflecting' the 'probable reliability' of the accounts with which I was dealing. When I allowed my judgement into my reporting – was I being less objective? Perhaps I was, in the sense that I was permitting my experience to influence my account of what I saw.

'We will lie to the world, but not to the President of the United States,' an Israeli official told me in Jerusalem when I was on my way a few weeks later to take up my post in Gaza permanently. The conversation, naturally, was for background information only, and this remark was made with a smile, but it illustrated very well the second broad question I want to discuss in relation to objectivity: how the reporter copes with outside influence. In all aspects of reporting – political, financial, consumer – journalists are put under pressure by public relations people to reflect one view or another (Davis, 2002; Davies, 2008). Perhaps because in war the stakes are often higher, that intention to manage or mislead becomes a complete lie, which, if wrongly repeated by the reporter, can have serious consequences for themselves, and for others. In wartime, the people seeking to exert pressure on the reporter may, as in the cases of financial or consumer journalism, be public relations consultants. They may more probably be government officials with a direct say in the kind of access a reporter will get, or, in more extreme circumstances, military or security personnel upon whom the journalist relies for their own safety. They may be in a position not only to withdraw any protection which is implicitly or explicitly offered by the presumed rules of the working relationship, but actually liable to threaten journalists whose work they do not like. So, when, as in the case of the Israeli official above, a government has decided to 'lie to the world' the correspondent's challenges as he or she decides how to report the information they receive are not simply those of weighing up competing claim and counterclaim, although that is the first and most pressing task in a journalistic sense. Maintaining that sense of objectivity can be much harder in a hostile environment than in the comfortable chair of a newsroom in London, New York or Paris. Fatigue, hunger and stress can all make it more difficult to make decisions – so striving for that ideal of balance, of giving equal weight to differing accounts, becomes all the harder.

Then there is the question of whether those differing accounts are sufficient in themselves. How much more information is needed to give a complete picture of an event? To return to the example of the destroyed factory mentioned above, it is difficult to argue that a description of the scene, combined with quotes from Palestinians and Israelis, could be considered a complete report. In one sense, it could. A journalist could have gone to the location, as I did, and sent a story outlining what they found there, adding the views of the protagonists. In another way, in the case of most conflicts, and in the case of the Israeli–Palestinian conflict in particular, this could have appeared woefully incomplete.

One of the basic rules of journalism holds that a reporter should always try to tell his or her audience why something happened. To answer this question at length in the case of an incident in wartime would usually leave no place for the news of the day itself. Naturally, when you are reporting for an audience familiar with the situation, there is often no need to go into too much detail. But most wars – especially those we report on today on today – have causes whose roots lie in history. The people who find themselves at the heart of the conflict are keenly aware of this. We have a duty to convey this to our audiences. As Carruthers has pointed out, the actual start of a war can often be a matter of dispute, 'Parties to a conflict often date its origins quite differently' (2000: 14).

Shortly after I arrived in Gaza, I interviewed a man whose home had been destroyed by the Israeli Army on the grounds that its location, close to an Israeli military post, meant that it could be used by Palestinian fighters as a firing position. Learning – through my colleague who was translating for me – that I was British, the man told me I was welcome in Gaza. He then admonished me for my country's past record as the once dominant power in the region. In particular, he was angry about the Balfour Declaration of 1917,[6] seen by many Palestinians as an important milestone towards the creation some three decades later of the state of Israel. If, more than eighty years on, the Balfour Declaration was still something in the daily thoughts of Palestinians as they considered their conflict with Israel, could a report omitting this historical context be considered complete, and therefore objective? There is no straightforward answer to this question – 'we're not here to give people a history lesson, after all' was a sentiment I heard expressed many times in BBC newsrooms – but no discussion of objectivity in conflict reporting can ignore it.

One frequent criticism of western reporting of the Israeli–Palestinian conflict is that it does not give sufficient prominence to the very fact of Israel's occupation of Gaza and the West Bank in 1967. The Glasgow University Media Group wrote of their work, 'The research showed that many people had little understanding of the reasons for the conflict and its origins' (Philo *et al.*, 2003: 134). That is not a lone example. How do we understand the wars in the former Yugoslavia in the 1990s without reference to history? How often did we who covered the wars in Chechnya refer to the Chechens' own deeply held and often mentioned conviction that Russia would attack them every time their population reached 1 million?[7] Sometimes, is the answer, but perhaps not enough. For whether or not it could be proved that Moscow's military strategy was driven by quite so precise a figure – and nothing has ever emerged to suggest that such a plan did exist – the fact that this belief was so widely held surely makes it instrumental in any attempt to shed light on why the Chechens feared the Russians, and the way in which they did so.

Context, then, is an important part of 'objectivity' – and context is not confined to reflecting historical factors in news reports. When a journalist acquires special knowledge of a conflict, usually through covering it in particular detail, or over a long period of time or both, they also acquire an authority. That authority allows them to offer analysis, or even informed speculation, on the present situation in a conflict, and what that might mean for its future course. I would argue that a reporter who has acquired that authority is not only right to use it, but has a duty to do so. This, of course, assumes that the journalist in question seeks to adhere to the principle of objectivity broadly outlined above. There are of course reporters who will willingly use their elevated position to act more as a propagandist for one side or another, even if they initially came to the war as an impartial observer. Sometimes this is born of a sense of moral duty, sometimes from political conviction. I'll look at the motivation of the journalist as propagandist a little later in the chapter. Here I want to assess the role of journalist as expert as it relates to ideas of objectivity.

Robert Fisk, the veteran Middle East correspondent, who currently works for the *Independent*, has often been sharply critical of both Israeli and western actions in the region. As a result, he has himself often been criticized. Whatever one might think of his reporting, Robert Fisk has followed the events in Lebanon, Israel and the Palestinian territories, Iraq, Iran and elsewhere for three decades and more – far longer, and in far greater detail (How long had Tony Blair or George Bush ever spent in Iraq before deciding to invade it? How many Palestinian refugee camps had either of them ever visited?) than those charged with taking policy decisions. The experienced reporter has earned a certain right to an audience. Just because the political leaders of that audience are uncomfortable with what the reporter might have to say does not mean that the reporter's work lacks objectivity. On the contrary: the fact that a journalist might better know what he or she is talking about than those who seek to criticise their work only serves to increase the journalist's authority. An objective report does not have to be a palatable one.

Martin Bell and the journalism of attachment

A decade and a half after it was published, Martin Bell's memoir *In Harm's Way* (1995) still has a central contribution to make to any discussion of objectivity in journalism. While some of his concerns about the way his trade was developing – such as his questioning whether a live broadcast from a correspondent whose report has just been aired can add much (1995: 66–7) – seem almost amusing to us now because they so blatantly contradict current trends, the debate which he started is still going on (Tumber, 2003: 255; Tumber and Prentoulis, 2003: 222; Carruthers, 2011: 158). Bell's long and varied career gave him an authority on theoretical questions which few could claim to match, and that ensured that his proposal attracted wide attention. It is harder to argue, though, that it actually led to change. The editorial policy of the BBC, in theory at least, is still to observe a much more traditional idea of objectivity: 'Our audiences need to be confident that the BBC's editorial decisions are not influenced by the outside activities or personal or commercial interests of programme makers or those who appear on air' (BBC Editorial Guidelines, 2010a). In conflicts where one side is much stronger than another in terms of troops or weapons, that becomes harder to do in practice.

In the way that ideas are often simplified in retelling or discussion, so Bell's original point seems to have been slightly lost. His definition of the journalism of attachment: 'It is not only knowing, but also caring' (1995: 128) has sometimes been portrayed as an argument for the abandonment of objectivity. It is not as straightforward as that. Bell is one of the most experienced conflict reporters of the last century, and, although Bosnia was the first war that moved him to write a book, he had clearly previously reflected on many of the issues he discusses. By his own admission, nothing had prepared Bell for the task which lay before him in Bosnia. He was working in a new kind of conflict – one ignited by the uncertainties of the post-Cold War world. His experience convinced him that this new kind of conflict required a new kind of journalism. Just a few pages after his definition of the journalism of attachment, Bell is keen to qualify what 'knowing, but also caring' means:

> Are we not all in some way interventionist? I suppose it is only human, in the midst of so much misery, to want to see an end to it. And I for one would gratefully hang up my body armour and my microphone, after Bosnia, absent myself from the war zones forever, and take up a post as peace correspondent (if such a job were to exist). But with the possible exception of the slightly polemical piece I did for *Panorama*[8] in the first year of the war, I have kept my feelings out of it. They have no business there. It is not the function of the reporter to campaign. That is for soldiers, politicians, or columnists. What we should be doing, or trying to do, is to show the situation on the ground, who is doing what to whom, and with what effects, and why.
>
> (ibid.: 142)

Bell knew what he was doing: using the authority of his experience to spark a debate on one of the most central beliefs of conflict journalism, by drawing attention to its potential shortcomings. As Tumber and Prentoulis have observed, 'In war/foreign corresponding, the rules of objectivity may restrict the ability of the correspondent to present the socio-political framework of a conflict, since he may be accused of "editorializing"' (2003: 221).

Anna Politkovskaya's reporting from Chechnya

Anna Politkovskaya, who had no peer as a chronicler of the war in Chechnya, was often accused of much worse. Her reporting of that conflict was almost certainly the reason for her murder in October 2006. The Russian authorities have so far failed to establish the full story of her death. There are few among the Russian military and political elite who would call her work 'objective', publicly at least. Until her death, Anna Politkovskaya continued to question the way that the war was being waged – not from any ideological conviction, but from a clear understanding, built from her unrivalled experience, that the Russian government's strategy in its restive southern region was not only murderous, but counterproductive.

In early 2002, she tells the story of a unit of Russian Federal troops (the 'Feds') as she refers to them, looting the Chechen village of Starye Atagi, and threatening its inhabitants. This is just one of many episodes she describes as she builds up a picture of widespread criminality among troops who are supposedly present in the region to wipe out groups of Chechen fighters.

> This time they also took money for women in Starye Atagi. As is customary in these places, prices for women were much lower than for me. And you paid for something different too: to avoid rape. The Feds took three hundred roubles from one family not to rape their young daughter, and five hundred roubles from another. They also took earrings and necklaces.
>
> Finally, the residents went out into the streets, lit fires, and stayed there every night. They hoped that being among other people could save them from death and rape. It did not save everyone.
>
> (2003: 105)

In case her readers are in any doubt about what conclusion they should draw from what they learn of the troops' behaviour – and we should remember that Politkovskaya's primary audience was a Russian one, in whose name this war was being conducted – she offers an analysis so clear that it reads like a threat. 'The only thing the methods of this war accomplish is to recruit new terrorists and resistance fighters, and to rouse hatred, calling for bloody revenge' (ibid.: 106).

There is no doubting Politkovskaya's implacable opposition to Russian policy in the North Caucasus. Does this mean her work lacks objectivity? No.

Her style is much more direct than that which one might for example hear on the BBC, or read in the *New York Times*, but I would argue that that is part of a wider Russian tradition of leaving little open to doubt in news reporting. The Russians have always looked to their writers as prophets and philosophers as well as storytellers, and part of this tradition seems to have transferred to journalism, too. Politkovskaya's work should be seen in that context. For not only does she challenge the official version of events that the government troops are there to bring stability, she demonstrates that their continuing presence is driven by their own desire not to renounce their own corrupt and highly lucrative economic activity.

> This is how things are done all over Chechnya. The officials' interest in the war is one of the biggest reasons for its continuation. The Khankala[9] generals (the North Caucasus United Group of Armies) and the general staff in Moscow are equally interested in the war continuing. Middle-rank officers stationed at the edge of Chechen villages make friends with minor local officials; neither of them want anyone to meddle in their small but gainful domain.
>
> (ibid.: 176)

Politkovskaya shows in detail how this racketeering affects the army at every level. It is a side of the Chechen war which western coverage failed adequately to reflect. Those of us who covered the conflict suspected it was going on. I remember one junior officer, who probably was not supposed to get on the journalists' bus in which I was travelling, describing at length how his regiment and one stationed nearby were battling for the lion's share of the illegal trade in their area. Some years later, a senior government official, during a briefing 'for background only' conceded that corruption among generals was the real reason that Moscow could not bring the war to an end. Politkovskaya understood this, and so told her readers why their sons were still being sent south to face a terrifying foe. Her angry opposition to the Kremlin's policy does not prevent her from reporting human suffering among the Russian troops, too. Their collective behaviour may be monstrous; that does not make them all monsters. She writes of an evening she spends in a hotel restaurant in Vladikavkaz[10] with a group of Russian servicemen. Her distress when she learns later that a Colonel among them has died of wounds is understated, but clear. Anna Politkovskaya wrote about the Chechen war with determination, perseverance and courage. If her despatches angered the Kremlin policy-makers, it was because her work threw light on Moscow's mistakes, and its lack of desire, or inability, to recognize them; not because they lacked objectivity. As Judith Lichtenberg writes, 'Between truth and falsehood the objective investigator is not neutral' (2000: 252).

The Chechen war killed countless combatants and civilians. The legitimate authority in the region, the Russian government, had no interest in trying to count the number of deaths, nor did it have the ability. The number of civilian deaths, had they been accurately recorded, would only have served to underline the amount of needless slaughter this war caused; an accurate count of military deaths, especially where many of those killed were conscripts whose families lacked the finance or influence to allow their sons to escape service, could have served to sap morale. In other words, there were clear political reasons for not giving a complete picture of the war.

Objectivity, images of violence and audiences

Any consideration of objectivity must also look at the issue of audiences' responses to images of violence. In Britain especially, it is a huge factor affecting editorial decisions. Many journalists returning from working in conflict zones, and answering the obvious question, 'What was it like?' will reply 'It's not like it was on TV.' British media are traditionally reluctant to show the true extent of death and injury in conflict zones. While it is acceptable to broadcast pictures of somebody firing a weapon, we rarely see the moment when the bullet hits its target. Both the BBC's Editorial Guidelines, and the Ofcom Programme Code, are clear, and express similar views, on what the viewer should see, and what they should not.

Here are two short extracts from the BBC's Editorial Guidelines. The first is from the section dealing with the portrayal of violence, the second on covering war.

> When real life violence, or its aftermath, is shown on television or reported on radio and online we need to strike a balance between the demands of accuracy and the dangers of desensitisation or unjustified distress.
>
> (BBC Editorial Guidelines, 2010d)

> We will respect human dignity without sanitising the realities of war, terror, emergencies and similar events. There must be clear editorial justification for the use of very graphic pictures.
>
> (BBC Editorial Guidelines, 2010e)

And here is an extract from the Ofcom Broadcasting Code Section 2, 'Harm and Offence':

> In applying generally accepted standards broadcasters must ensure that material which may cause offence is justified by the context (see

meaning of 'context' below). Such material may include, but is not limited to, offensive language, violence, sex, sexual violence, humiliation, distress, violation of human dignity, discriminatory treatment or language (for example on the grounds of age, disability, gender, race, religion, beliefs and sexual orientation). Appropriate information should also be broadcast where it would assist in avoiding or minimising offence.

(Ofcom, 2011)[11]

In 2010, Ofcom found Al-Jazeera English (AJE) to be in breach of this rule for pictures they broadcast of a news item in which 'a number of people appeared to be shown being forced to lie down and then being shot dead by Nigerian security forces' (Ofcom, 2010). Other parts of the world see things differently. When I was covering the Israeli–Palestinian conflict in Gaza, I was shocked by the bloody images broadcast on Palestinian television. The purpose was obviously to remind the audience – although in this case it hardly needed it – of the death and suffering inflicted by Israeli forces in the Palestinian territories. As a television viewer in Russia too, I became used to seeing far more graphic pictures, not just of conflict, but also of murders and road accidents than would be normal in the west. Part of this comes down to different ideas of how taste and decency, and the need to avoid 'sanitising the realities of war', should affect editorial decision-making.

Which approach is best? The distressing images of dead and wounded children shown on television in Gaza and elsewhere in the Arab world, as well as showing death in wartime as it is, also traumatized and terrified children whose journey to school could on some days put them in mortal danger. They did not need reminding. In the west, we face a different dilemma. It is worth noting that neither the BBC Guidelines nor the Ofcom Code actually bans the airing of graphic war footage, they just specify it must be justified. In reality, such images are rarely shown. The result is what Daya Thussu has called, 'war as infotainment: the obsession with hi-tech reporting, using a video game format to present combat operations, with complex graphics and satellite imagery, providing a largely virtual, even bloodless, coverage of war' (2003: 117).

The finest editors are inspired by sound judgement, not governed by rules. Showing blood and guts all the time will eventually mean it loses its impact, or its audience or both. Never showing it means we fail to report what is happening. In a world where policy-makers so often seem oblivious of the civilian casualties in wars which they start, news organizations can make a case for showing – sometimes – what their reporters see. It might even ensure that presidents and prime ministers have a better idea of what is happening where their troops are fighting if they are able to see it close up, even if the close-ups are only of the camera kind. The people who elected those presidents and prime ministers, the people whose taxes are paying for the military campaigns, surely have a right to see too.

Capturing Saddam Hussein – a study in journalistic objectivity

The capture of Saddam Hussein in December 2003 was a news story which the US troops occupying Iraq, and their civilian masters, wanted, and needed, desperately. They had invaded Iraq almost nine months earlier and still Saddam Hussein was neither dead nor captured. I was in Baghdad at the time on a temporary assignment from my then base in Gaza. On the morning of Sunday 14 December, rumours began to circulate that he had been caught. A Coalition Provisional Authority (CPA, the civilian leadership of the occupying forces) news conference was announced for the afternoon. 'Does this mean we can go home early?' American soldiers asked the journalists as they searched them when they arrived for the event. Inside, the leader of the CPA, Paul Bremmer began the news conference with the words: 'Ladies and gentlemen, we got him.' A group of Iraqi journalists rose to their feet and began applauding. Some non-Iraqi reporters joined in the celebrations. Those who didn't still realized that they had a huge story on their hands – one which they had been waiting for since the invasion the previous spring. For the US administration, the wait had in a sense been even longer. It went back to September 11. So the capture became 'a moment to reinvigorate American nationalism in a post-Cold War era, a time of fragmented and fractured identities,' as Silvio Waisbord (2002: 206) said of September 11 itself. In such circumstances, for those who willingly celebrated, 'journalism was a mobilizer of national identity' (ibid.: 206).

Mr Bremmer's words had an air of spontaneity, but must, of course, have been carefully prepared. They were chosen to make the perfect headline, an easy excerpt to include at the very beginning of broadcast programmes around the world. Despite the fact that Saddam Hussein had been captured the previous evening, the news conference took place in the afternoon, ensuring that the news was still fresh when the East Coast of the United States awoke shortly afterwards.

For those Iraqi journalists who jumped for joy when they heard the news, objectivity was clearly not an issue. For the rest of us, try as we might, we found ourselves largely confined to reporting only the CPA's version of events, one it completely controlled. It timed the announcement of the story itself, and it showed the TV pictures of Saddam Hussein receiving a medical examination after his capture. It was the afternoon. It was winter, and nightfall was not far away. The village near Tikrit where Hussein had been captured was an estimated four hours away by roads unsafe for citizens of countries involved in the invasion. Although at least one western reporter did make the journey then, others were tied to Baghdad by countless, imminent deadlines and safety concerns. Problems of 'access' which I discussed in the preceding chapter all came into play – the absence of multiple sources, combined with the risks involved in seeking them, made this an example of 'controlled reporting', even if the journalists covering the story were in theory free to go where they wished. The result was that it was impossible to establish objectively, with any certainty, anything about this story beyond the fact that Saddam Hussein was in the hands of the invaders. The occupying authorities' control of the news was so complete that reporters were reduced to conveying little more than their version of events.

On that single day, that was not perhaps so serious. But I have always felt that one of a correspondent's most important tasks is to try to explain to his or her audience what the longer-term consequences of an event might be. In the absence of the voices of those who might have wanted Saddam Hussein to return to power in Iraq, this was very hard to do. And it was important to do it because, only months later, beginning in April the following year, they would unleash a powerful counter-attack on the occupiers. Audiences outside Iraq could have gained the impression from some of the coverage that day that this was some kind of conclusive moment in the invading coalition's military campaign in Iraq. It was not. It was undoubtedly a triumph for the coalition, especially in propaganda terms, but audiences probably inferred that its strategic significance was greater than it really was.

The next day, questions of access and objectivity conspired again against comprehensive reporting. My BBC colleagues and I travelled north of Baghdad to the place where Saddam Hussein had been captured. We found the location without difficulty, then were forced to wait a few hundred metres away for four or five hours. During this time, we watched groups of people arriving and departing by helicopter: among them, apparently, journalists 'embedded' with the US 4th

Infantry Division, which was based nearby. Our punishment for not being embedded was to be kept at arm's length while our competitors got their material first. Carruthers's description of the pooling arrangements which the US forces had put in place during the 1991 Gulf War, reminded me strongly of what had happened that day. 'Journalists of other nationalities, and less fortunate British, French and American journalists representing smaller, or more critical, outlets were consigned to the second tier (a few rungs lower down the Pentagon-devised journalistic evolutionary ladder)' (2000: 134–5).

The technique had perhaps even been made more efficient – from the authorities' point of view – in the intervening years (and this in comparison to what Alex Thomson called 'the largest operation in media control we have seen in recent years' (1992: ix). Even my status as the reporter from the main news broadcaster of an ally, a broadcaster with a massive international as well as British reach, did not allow me to advance upwards by even a single rung.

Our location, close to the village, did enable us to talk, through a fence, to some of the local people: 'Why did he surrender and not become a martyr?' and 'If we had known he was there, we would have fought for him!' were typical statements – the latter especially pertinent in view of the insurgency that was to come the following spring. I did my best – on a day made difficult by an impossibly large number of deadlines (naturally); bad weather; security concerns; and very poor communications, to try to relay some of this: but overall this was an event where cool-headed assessment of what happened was marginalized by the triumphalism of the coalition, and lack of access to alternative voices. This was not an example of objectivity in conflict reporting so much as one of the difficulty of attaining it.

Reporting based on a limited amount of information does not always lead to bad journalism, or poor writing. I make the case simply that some of the coverage of Saddam Hussein's capture and its immediate aftermath was irresponsibly incomplete.

John Reed: the reporter as propagandist

The American journalist John Reed, whose *Ten Days That Shook the World* (1977) is the definitive and enduring reporter's account of the 1917 Russian revolution, is perhaps not an account of war reporting in the conventional sense, but I want to look at it here for two reasons: first, because the urban warfare among a civilian population which he describes has plenty of parallels in our more recent history (think of Grozny, Gaza, Baghdad or Misrata), and, second, for what his book tells us about the reporter as propagandist. For Reed was a committed Communist who shared the ideals of the Bolsheviks whose seizure of power he chronicled. He describes Lenin speaking to his supporters in the days following the revolution on 7 November.

> Suddenly, by common impulse, we found ourselves on our feet, mumbling together into the smooth lifting unison of the *Internationale*. A grizzled old soldier was sobbing like a child. Alexandra Kollontai[12] rapidly winked the tears back. The immense sound rolled through the hall, burst windows and doors and soared into the quiet sky. 'The war is ended! The war is ended!' said a young workman near me, his face shining.
>
> (1977: 133)

Nor does Reed limit his support to the revolutionary cause to uplifting renditions of socialist anthems. Travelling with a group of troops loyal to the Bolsheviks, he doesn't think twice about taking a weapon, 'Arms were distributed to us, revolvers and rifles – "we might meet some Cossacks,[13] you know" – and we all piled into the ambulance, together with three great bundles of newspapers for the front' (ibid.: 208).

As his journey continues, Reed shares with us a picture of a city in the midst of armed conflict: the division between civilian and combatant indistinct, as often in our age; Reed's determination to make simple heroes of the people whose ideals he so passionately shared perfectly clear:

> We sped out on the wide, straight highway, grey with the first light fall of snow. It was thronged with Red Guards, stumbling along on foot towards the revolutionary front, shouting and singing; others, grey-faced and muddy, coming back. Most of them seemed to be mere boys. Women with spades, some with rifles and bandoliers, others wearing the Red Cross on their arm-bands, the bowed, toil-worn, women of the slums.
>
> (ibid.)

Conclusion: the challenges of understanding objectivity, and why objectivity matters

Susan Carruthers's reflection that reporters can be 'dependent on elite approval for access to the corridors of power' (2011: 43), highlights one of the pervading political forces which militates against objectivity. Judith Lichtenberg adds 'another of the standard criticisms of journalism's commitment to objectivity: not that it necessarily favours established power, but that it leads to a destructive agnosticism and scepticism' (ibid.: 251). Lichtenberg's conclusion that 'these criticisms ... suffer from too mechanical a conception of objectivity' (ibid.) reflects the challenges that exist even in attempting to define objectivity. As Robinson *et al.* observe, 'Political communication scholarship has long been sensitive to the difficulties surrounding terms such as *objectivity* and *bias*. The use of such terms often triggers accusations of modernist conceptions of the truth being available and identifiable' (2010: 8). These are legitimate concerns in scholarship, but they do not reduce the value of objectivity – as defined for the purposes of this chapter – as a professional value: something to be used as a guiding principle for reporting. Part of that idea of objectivity is context – crucially important, and too often absent. As Greg Philo's research led him to conclude,

> TV audiences have in general very little understanding of events in the developing world or of major international institutions or relationships. This is in part the result of TV coverage which tends to focus on dramatic, violent and tragic images while giving very little context or explanation to the events which are being portrayed.
>
> (2004: 222)

This lack of context was what undermined the coverage of the capture of Saddam Hussein. The presence of context – a determination to use as many sources, and reflect as many views, as possible – is what made Anna Politkovskaya's reporting from Chechnya so valuable, even if her work challenged some traditional notions of objectivity. Because of his own commitment, John Reed's account of the Russian revolution, stirring as it may be, does not give a full picture. That is the end to which we must work as journalists; objectivity is often the means.

Reed would presumably have conveyed with great enthusiasm, and in the first-person plural, the news that 'We got him!' That is, if the declaration referred to the Russian tsar. Reed's dedication to the cause would make government officials in today's world envious and, were they to reflect on his account, it might inspire them by its enthusiasm, if not its Bolshevik ideology. Increasingly in the sphere of modern conflict, governments at war are devoting huge amounts of resources to getting reporters on their side: an issue I look at in detail next.

Summary

- objectivity a central idea in all conflict journalism
- an objective journalist strives to keep their political and religious views, professional allegiances and financial interests from influencing their reporting
- issues relating to the concept of objectivity: the challenges of applying these principles when reporting from a conflict zone, context, taste and decency
- Martin Bell and the journalism of attachment
- Anna Politkovskaya's reporting from Chechnya
- objectivity and images of violence
- the capture of Saddam Hussein as a news event
- the journalist as propagandist: John Reed's *Ten Days That Shook the World*

4 How the war was spun: the role of public relations companies, propagandists and governments

Since the start of human conflict, belligerents have had, alongside their soldiers, armour and weapons, their advocates and apologists. Nations and political movements fighting wars seek to influence public opinion in order to further their cause, and to do down that of their foes.

In our world, where the global political power blocs which shaped the Cold War have disappeared or shifted, and where technology brings new opportunities to warring forces both on and off the battlefield, public relations tactics are evolving too. In some cases, they are taking on an unprecedented importance. Most of this chapter will focus on my research into the role that public relations played in the reporting of the war between Russia and Georgia in 2008. First, though, I would like briefly to consider some existing studies of PR in wartime.

Studies of propaganda in conflict reporting

Herman and Chomsky's *Manufacturing Consent* (1994) continues to provoke, enrage and influence to the same extent as when it was first published in the 1980s. Some have criticized it as oversimplistic – Schudson, for example, dismisses its 'flat-footed functionalism' (2000: 180). Whether or not one agrees with its idea of a 'propaganda model' (Herman and Chomsky, 1994: 1) which controls news journalism, its analysis of the coverage of the Vietnam War appears prescient in its anticipation of some of the issues which would later cause controversy in the reporting of the invasion of Iraq. One of the five 'news "filters"' (ibid.: 2) identified by Herman and Chomsky is 'anticommunism as a control mechanism' (ibid.: 29). 'This ideology helps mobilize the populace against an enemy, and because the concept is fuzzy it can be used against anybody advocating policies that threaten property interests or support accommodation with Communist states and radicalism' (ibid.: 29). It is impossible to read this without thinking of the 'fuzzy' 'concept' that was the United States' 'war on terror'. As Carruthers observes, George W. Bush,

administration officials and supportive opinion-formers developed this parallel by casting the 'war on terror' as an epoch-making struggle against 'Islamofascism' – a dangerous, militant, ideology on the march worldwide, preying on the disadvantaged and deluded, just as communism had in the late 1940s and 1950s.

(2011: 199)

Also writing about Vietnam, Daniel Hallin (1989) highlights 'the ideology of the Cold War' (1989: 24) as one of two factors upon which the US president's power to control foreign affairs news in the early 1960s rested. The second, he says, 'was professional journalism itself' (ibid.: 25). 'The assumptions and routines of what is often known as "objective journalism" made it exceedingly easy for officials to manipulate day-to-day news content' (ibid.). This combination of political influence and vulnerability to what we now call 'spin' remains a threat to good reporting, as I will show later in this chapter.

In the post-September 11 age, Robin Brown has written, 'Mobilizing, informing, and persuading are integral to the conduct of war. The result is that attempting to shape the representation of the conflicts becomes more important for the belligerents even as it becomes harder to do' (2003: 89). Yes, and no – after all, other researchers make the case that new communication technologies have not necessarily made it harder to control media coverage. As Robinson *et al.* suggest, 'increasingly professional government media-management techniques may have been effective in countering these developments' (2010: 29).

At this point, I think it would be useful to define the phrase 'information warfare' as I feel it should be understood in discussion of contemporary conflict reporting. For me, 'information warfare' comprises two distinct, but related, concepts:

1   combat in the information age, involving extensive use of information technology in weapons and communications;
2   attempts by the belligerents to influence to their strategic advantage the way that the conflict in which they are involved is reported.

For the purposes of this chapter, I will concentrate on the second meaning. Tumber and Webster's even broader definition is also helpful in understanding a complex concept. 'We intend to use the concept Information War to invoke much more than technologies. For us, it also entails a series of connected social, political, and economic factors' (2006: 1).

Russia and Georgia's war of August 2008

In August 2008, as the world settled into sofas, bar stools or around the tables of tea shops to watch the start of the Olympic Games in Beijing, Russia and Georgia went to war. As the BBC's correspondent in Moscow, I covered the conflict. That week, I reported from the Russian capital on the Russian authorities' version of events, and their actions and reactions as diplomatic attempts to end the fighting got underway. Two years earlier, I had spent a week in Georgia, my time divided almost equally between covering a referendum in South Ossetia, one of the separatist regions whose future status lay at the heart of the conflict, and trips to Georgian military facilities in parts of the country which were under the control of the central government in Tbilisi. A few weeks after the outbreak of war, with the situation much calmer, I returned to South Ossetia on a brief visit for journalists organized by the Russian Army. Shortly after that, I returned to Tbilisi to talk to officials there. David Edmonds and I were making a programme, *The PR Battle for the Caucasus* (Rodgers and Edmonds, 2008), about the role of public relations consultants in the conflict. The aim was to try to determine how important the media campaign – fought with all the technological tools the sides could lay their hands on – had been in the war. 'In this century, and in a conflict where you have a huge power against a small state, I think that's almost as important as the military battle' (ibid.), Shota Utiashvili, an official with the Georgian interior ministry, told me. His words were a confirmation of a public relations war of unprecedented extent which had been underway during the conflict itself.

Both Russia and Georgia employed western public relations companies to promote their version of events. Their purpose was not just to form and influence opinion of the conflict. It was to establish as true a sequence of events which showed their paymasters in a more favourable light than their enemies. Because their role was – in one case at least – to try to persuade journalists that things that had not happened had taken place, it is worth outlining a brief, generally accepted version of events.

On the night of 7–8 August 2008, heavy fighting broke out in the Georgian separatist region of South Ossetia. Over the next couple of days, Russian troops, supporting separatist fighters, drove Georgian Army units out of South Ossetia, then advanced further into Georgia. A week later, President Nicolas Sarkozy of France, which then held the rotating presidency of the European Union, brokered a ceasefire, bringing an end to the fighting. Russian troops remained in South Ossetia, and in another separatist region, Abkhazia. Shortly afterwards, Russia recognized both territories as independent states. At the time of writing, Georgia remains determined that South Ossetia and Abkhazia should be returned to its control, albeit with a great deal of autonomy, but it is very difficult to see how this could happen. The origins of the conflict go back to the break-up of the Soviet Union, two decades ago. There is no undisputed version of how this brief war actually started. Russia and Georgia both remain adamant that the other was the aggressor.

The origins of the public relations war go back more than two years before the first shot was fired in August 2008. In 2006, Russia held the presidency of the G8 group of industrialized countries. That year's G8 summit, held in July in St Petersburg, the native city of the then Russian president, Vladimir Putin, was supposed to be a splendid affair, demonstrating that Russia was once again a global power, and not the corrupt, impoverished weakling of a state which had initially emerged from the collapse of the USSR. There was one problem. While the rest of the world agreed that Russia was once more a force in global affairs, many saw little to admire. Mr Putin had presided over impressive economic growth, and a more stable society, but his critics contended that these gains had come at the expense of political and media freedom, and human rights. Mr Putin's administration did not want this to be the story of the summit – so they turned to western experts to seek advice on how to handle the western media. The US-based public relations company, Ketchum, won the contract to lead a consortium of companies to help Russia tell its story. GPlus, a Brussels-based political communications consultancy, took the lead in dealing with European journalists. This relationship was still going strong at the time of the war with Georgia in 2008. When that conflict broke out, there seemed little doubt that Russia would soon prevail. Even though Georgia had increased its defence budget in the years since 2003, its largely untried army was never likely to be a match for the overwhelming numbers and fire power at the disposal of its neighbour and former political master. Realizing that military defeat was inevitable, Georgia settled for telling a story other than martial glory.

'There's only one question that matters in the end, which is who started the war' said James Hunt, a founding partner of Aspect, a consultancy also based in Brussels (Rodgers and Edmonds, 2008). At the time the conflict erupted, his company was advising Georgia on its bid to join NATO. I interviewed him for the BBC a few weeks later.

And what we've tried to do throughout the whole process is to demonstrate that Russia's actions, accumulated actions over weeks and months ahead of August 7th, combined with their evacuation of Tskhinvali[14] and their use then of the South Ossetian irregulars to shell Georgian villages on the nights of the 5th and 6th of August all add up to, in effect, a declaration of war by Russia on Georgia.

That is the issue that lies at the heart of the public relations executives' attempts to influence international opinion in favour of their clients. They took their contest to new levels. The warring sides, especially Russia, went to unprecedented lengths, and expended vast resources, to try to portray themselves as morally superior in a conflict which, in the end, did neither side much credit. Once the fighting started, the PR companies joined battle too, like expensive mercenaries paid huge sums to achieve what the protagonists' armed forces could not manage alone. Georgia seemed, initially, to have the upper hand. For the Russians, that served to confirm their belief that it was Georgia who had planned and started the conflict.

'Well for Russians it was unprepared war,' Andrei Klimov, a member of the Russian parliament for the majority 'United Russia' party, told me (ibid.).

Georgia hired some special agencies, paid them money since November last year. And they prepared for any variation of event: we, not. It was vacation period. It was empty city Moscow. We were not prepared for this. We prepared for the Olympic Games, but not for this conflict. And we lost at least five days for our reaction.

(ibid.)

Five days is probably an exaggeration. As the war unfolded to the south, Russia's politicians led their campaign from the capital. Less than thirty-six hours after they began to prove their supremacy on the battlefield, they realized they needed to change tactics in the information war. It happened very quickly. In my office in Moscow that Saturday morning, 9 August, I received an email inviting me to take part in a conference call for correspondents with the Russian foreign minister, Sergei Lavrov. I accepted. A short while afterwards, though, that offer was superseded by one of an individual interview with Mr Lavrov in the foreign ministry. Mine was the first of three or four he gave to foreign broadcasters that day. I first went to work in Moscow as a journalist in 1991, and never had I experienced such speedy and efficient granting of access to senior decision-makers. I tried later, while making the programme about the role of public relations in the conflict, to establish exactly who had taken the decision to be so much more open. No one who knew would give me an official answer to the question, but one very good source familiar with the situation told me it had come 'from the top': in other words, either from President Dmitry Medvedev, or the prime minister, and at the time, Russia's most powerful politician, Vladimir Putin. In either case, the initiative originated at the very highest level of the Russian elite.

Getting to talk to senior officials is rarely easy for foreign journalists in Russia. For international broadcasters working in English, that challenge is further complicated by editors' desire, insistence even, to get English-speaking contributors wherever possible. From that Saturday morning onwards, they seemed to appear on demand. Many, including Mr Klimov, whom I quoted above, were apparently summoned back to Moscow to take part in this great push for PR victory. On the following Monday morning, 11 August, I was invited to a meeting in the Kremlin to discuss the BBC's requirements for English-speaking Russian officials in the coming days.

Russia's media mobilization did not mean that Georgia was driven onto the defensive. On the contrary, the Georgians seemed to redouble their efforts. 'I counted the number of telephone interviews I gave. It was one thousand, one hundred,' Shota Utiashvili, the Georgian interior ministry official later told me (ibid.). Even President Mikheil Saakashvili himself seemed to be almost constantly on air on international news channels, to the extent that one might have begun to wonder whether that was the best use of the head of state's time during war. If Georgia had any hope that the US might decide to come to its assistance (Mr Saakashvili's administration was at that time especially close to that of the former US president, George W. Bush) that soon proved to be completely misplaced. Georgia was on its own as far as troops and tanks were concerned. Presumably having realized that it was facing a certain rout on the battlefield, Georgia strove instead for a moral victory in the media. Its mercenaries on the civilized boulevards of Brussels – the headquarters of both agencies are only a few streets apart in the Belgian capital – a world away from the heat, blood and agony of a Caucasus war zone in August, were pressed into action too. 'I suppose at the height of the war on August 8th, 9th, we were probably sending out an email every hour, every 90 minutes,' James Hunt from Aspect recalled a few weeks later (ibid.).

In the PR war's most intense moments, the tactics began to evolve. They moved from seeking to influence opinion to seeking to report what had actually taken place: not just trying to tell journalists what to think, but actually trying to establish themselves as a news source.

The fate of the Georgian town of Gori lay at the centre of this. Gori, famous prior to the conflict mainly as the birthplace of the twentieth-century dictator Joseph Stalin, was significant because it lay beyond the administrative border dividing South Ossetia from the rest of Georgia. If the Russian Army were to advance into Gori, it would suggest that its campaign in Georgia had a wider objective than simply driving the Georgian Army out of South Ossetia. It might even suggest that it was preparing to advance on the Georgian capital, Tbilisi, and depose President Saakashvili. It was very difficult to determine what was happening in and around the city. One of the three journalists killed covering this conflict would be killed in Gori three days later; others had close escapes. Some were quite seriously injured. It was not an easy place to gather reliable information. James Hunt and his PR colleagues put themselves forward in an attempt to fill that void, distributing as fact information which they could not themselves confirm, as he admitted to me later: 'You do get confused information, there's no two ways about that. We here in Brussels put a lot of pressure on your organization, the BBC, and on CNN to say you should change the tickers on your screen because the Russians have taken Gori' (ibid.). James Hunt, speaking two months later, felt that the fact that the Russians did take Gori a day or so afterwards justified his decision to put pressure on journalists. Few journalists would agree. Any who chose to report that information without at the very least qualifying the source would have been failing their audiences, and, irrespective of their distance from the fighting itself, failing to do their job.

The implications of PR's attempts to influence conflict reporting

This reliance on public relations material is neither entirely new, nor is it limited to conflict reporting. What is new is the extent to which it is proliferating, both in conflict reporting, and in other areas of journalism. In his important and widely praised book, *Flat Earth News: An Award-winning Reporter Exposes Falsehood, Distortion, and Propaganda in the Global Media* (2008), Nick Davies makes a detailed and convincing case that PR companies are driving, or at least greatly influencing, the agendas of major news organizations. His opinion of these companies is not high: 'fabrication is at the heart of PR', he tells us (2008: 165). He has countless examples to back up his claim, some of which are very similar to my experiences of dealing with PR firms during the Russia–Georgia war of 2008. Where I uncovered deliberate attempts by Georgia's PR agents to mislead journalists as to the fate of the city of Gori, Davies documents the work of Sam Gardiner, a former Colonel in the US Air Force, who conducted a detailed study of the way that the governments of the US and Britain presented the conflict to journalists, and thus, to their populations.

Gardiner is clear that these are not the kind of errors that can easily be explained away by misleading mutterings about the fog of war. Gardiner's paper, 'Truth from These Podia' (2003) begins 'It was not bad intelligence. It was much more. It was an orchestrated effort. It began before the war, was a major effort during the war, and continues as post-conflict distortions' (2003: 3).

This kind of orchestrated effort was exactly what I encountered in my reporting of the Russia–Georgia war, and in the programme I made afterwards about the public relations companies' role in it. Nick Davies talks about the US use of what it calls 'strategic communications'. 'Its chief architect is the Pentagon,' he writes, 'which has succeeded in engineering a significant expansion of its own ability to manipulate information as a weapon' (2008: 235).

Davies is not alone in identifying this as a significant development in the US post-September 11 strategy. Robin Brown too has written about it in the following terms,

> In waging the war on terrorism, the United States has made use of three different paradigms of communications as a tool of influence: military concepts of information warfare, foreign policy concepts of public diplomacy, and approaches to media management drawn from domestic politics.
>
> (2003: 90)

Both Brown and Davies mention the case of the planned creation of the 'Office of Strategic Influence' in the United States following the attacks of September 11 2001. The plans were leaked, and the new office was disbanded almost as it came into being. Abandoning the office, however, did not mean abandoning the idea: as Gardiner, Davies, Brown and my own experience have all shown. 'Information operations', as military attempts to influence the news agenda in the hope of gaining advantage in conflict are known, are now one of the faces of modern warfare. Gardiner, whom I interviewed by email for this book, remains adamant that the 'Office of Strategic Influence' disappeared in name only. 'Most certainly the office went away,' he told me,

> but the effort continued very vigorously. I don't believe I can point to a conflict where the leadership in the Pentagon and White House spent so much time on attempts to influence US and global public opinion. It was their main effort.
>
> (Email, 4 November 2010)

One episode in the Iraq war which Gardiner examines at length is the uncertainty over the fate of the Iraqi city of Basra. Had it fallen as reported? Gardiner demonstrates that the capture of the city was constructed as a media 'fact' long before it actually took place. The similarity with the confusion over the fate of Gori, discussed above, is striking.

'The comparison is very valid,' Gardiner observes. 'The fall of the first two cities in Iraq had been planned way in advance to be one of the first positive stories of the invasion. They got carried away telling the story' (ibid.).

As in Iraq, so in Georgia: the spin doctors got 'carried away', and, as they took off on their flight of wishful thinking, they did their best to take as many members of the news media as possible along for the ride.

I suggested in Chapter 1 that two factors above all others have influenced conflict reporting: politics, and technology. Susan Carruthers has neatly expressed the views of those who believe the first – with the wider definition I would like to give it for the purposes of this book – is especially relevant.

> To look at which wars media cover, for how long, and in what ways, is less to see a recognisable reflection of the 'world as it is' – as journalists are wont to claim – than a map of the broad preoccupations, interests, and values of their particular society.
>
> (2000: 7)

Changing technology, and our post-Cold War, post-September 11 global political situation, have created a whole new media space, and a whole new set of policy priorities. Unfortunately, they have also created a whole new set of traps for journalists. The phrase 'information war' in this case also encompasses an additional meaning: the battle which journalists have to fight to try to get information untainted by the hands of political spin doctors, or PR advisors. As James Hunt told me in his approach to promoting Georgia's view in the war with Russia, they are ready to put 'a lot of pressure' on news organizations to report their point of view. The problem for journalists is that this pressure is all too often effective. In the case of South Ossetia, Russia may have joined the PR war after the main conflict was underway, but, just as it was sending its troops into Georgian territory, the Georgian government, via its advocates in Brussels, was trying to seize the commanding heights in the news battlefield. Russia knew it had to enter the conflict there, too, or the expected military victory, when it came, would have been of much less value.

Russia arguably started from a disadvantaged position, which was the opposite of its clear advantage in conventional military terms. For the onset of the conflict was often reported in terms harking back to the Cold War, creating an image of a Russia which is alien, uncivilized, violent and unpredictable. Bears emerged from the depths of some imaginary Siberian forest to populate newspaper cartoons. This latent Russophobia showed how very difficult a job the PR consultants hired by the Kremlin had had in the preceding two years, and now a single news story – albeit one that was both sensational and significant – was undoing any gains they had achieved.

'I think they got spooked because Saakashvili was doing so well. He was everywhere, and the initial reporting tended to spin it in the Georgian way,' recalls Angus Roxburgh, a former BBC Moscow correspondent who, at the time of the war, was working for GPlus (Interview, London, 30 September 2010).

Asked if there was a sense that the information war was an important part of the conflict as a whole, and Russia had to get involved, he replies,

Absolutely, because they were definitely appalled at the idea that they were being blamed for the whole thing, and so they felt vindicated when the Tagliavini[15] report came out that at least sort of equally shared the blame, certainly said that the Georgians had started it on the night, whatever the provocations had been. They really didn't like the idea that the Georgians were getting the better of them on that, and they felt they were.

(ibid.)

Looking back, two years later, Roxburgh agreed that it would be fair to say that this was a western game which the Russian administration did not fully comprehend, but one in which they knew they had to participate.

They didn't really understand it. We taught them what we could, but they came into it with strange ideas about how the western press worked.[16] I think they felt that everybody else did do it, that all other governments had PR people working for them as well – but didn't completely understand it.

(ibid.)

Roxburgh's conclusion seems to suggest that this western model of wartime news management is not universally effective but, when the information war is being fought in the international – i.e. largely western – media, then it becomes the norm.

Georgia seemed to suffer from no such uncertainty. Georgia had cannily played to what strengths it had. As a result, western politicians lined up to condemn Russia's actions without seeking to understand the more complex and disputed reasons behind Russia's invasion of South Ossetia. David Cameron, leader of the British Conservative Party, which was then in opposition, travelled to Georgia. In an article for the *Sunday Times,* he declared, referring to an upmarket department store in London popular with foreign visitors, including Russians, 'Russian armies can't march into other countries while Russian shoppers carry on marching into Selfridges' (Cameron, 2008).

The new world of continuous news demanded an instant response from political leaders, as well as from the news media. More considered reflections later would make some political acts, and some reporting, appear hasty. Nevertheless, belligerents, leaders of third countries, and journalists all knew they had to engage in this third definition of information war – a kind of fight for resources – in which latecomers might miss their chance of being heard, and, with it, their chance of influence. Each news bulletin demanded something *new* and the public relations people were on hand to promote it: for the Georgians, the premature capture of Gori; for the Russians an oft-repeated and never substantiated claim that 2,000 people had been killed in the Georgian Army's initial advance into South Ossetia, and that the deaths there amounted to 'genocide' (Ministry of Foreign Affairs of the Russian Federation, 2008). The media were treated like children grasping crayons, and with a blank sheet of paper on the table in front of them: desperate to draw, but lacking inspiration for a subject – until the PR people stepped forward gently to guide their hand.

This approach appears as a refined version of an earlier technique – updated for use in a new media landscape. As Brown notes, in his chapter in 'War and the Media', this kind of tactic was behind one of the enduring television images of the 1991 war in Iraq,

> The classic example in recent times was the provision to the media in the 1991 Gulf War of videotapes of precision guided missiles hitting their targets with uncanny accuracy, thus deflecting media attention away from the fact that 90 per cent of coalition bombing was with old-fashioned 'dumb' weapons.
>
> (2003: 104)

These efforts by governments and their agents are a new version of a timeless attempt to influence. Stephen Somerville was Reuters bureau chief in Saigon during the Vietnam War. In an interview for this book, he recalled of JUSPAO (the Joint United States Public Affairs Office),

> It was quite sophisticated. They had what you've no doubt heard of, the 'Five o'clock follies', the daily briefing by a senior American official which took place at the communications headquarters, the JUSPAO headquarters, and some correspondents made a point of never going. But most did because there was always something you could pick up even though it was very much the official line.
>
> (Interview, London, 17 May 2011)

Writing of a conflict a generation later, the 1991 Gulf War, Alex Thomson suggests that the briefings reporters got then 'were more informed' (1992: 99), but notes importantly, 'the great advantage reporters in Vietnam had was almost unlimited mobility with the US forces' (ibid.: 98), an ease of access which Somerville also remembered.

Today's version of news management in wartime takes advantage of the fact that, as in South Ossetia, journalists are kept away until it suits the combatants. The PR warriors have a good understanding of how twenty-four-hour news works. Journalism has always been about being first, but never more so than now. Even fifteen years ago, you might have a few hours to consider a story, check it, seek extra sources and confirmation, before running it and still be 'first': no longer. While the traditional television news bulletins have retained an influence which some predicted they would have lost by now, almost all major news organizations have an outlet for breaking news too. Taking the time to weigh up claim and counterclaim before six or ten o'clock is no longer a possibility. Sitting on a potentially significant development for more than a few seconds could mean losing out to the opposition, a chance that news organizations are never keen to take. The pressure is on to err on the side of risk.

The BBC World Service continues to insist that every story is either reported on two independent sources, or from one of their own correspondents. This kind of rigour has all but disappeared elsewhere. Even within other parts of the BBC, recent years have seen a discussion of the idea of 'emerging truth'. On the face of it, it is a reasonable proposition that, as the facts of any breaking story become available, there are likely to be contradictions and omissions. In practice, it often seemed to mean that broadcasting an unconfirmed report from a single source was fine, provided you identified it as such. There are many occasions when this is true, provided a journalist has weighed up the likelihood of the report being reliable enough to merit running. Simply to report every news agency wire which seems potentially newsworthy, though, is to fail your audience. Other journalists among that audience may appreciate what it means to source a report to a specific news agency – non-journalists are much more likely to recall only where they read or saw the news.

In that kind of culture, in reporting conflict, as in other branches of journalism, the news organizations' defences against the PR warriors are weak. As so often in warfare, it is the civilians, in this case, audiences, which suffer most. This is especially true where unsubstantiated claims are made at a time calculated to have great impact, and then not later checked or corrected.

I mentioned above the Russian claim that 2,000 civilians were killed in the initial Georgian advance into South Ossetia. It was given great prominence in the Russian media, and frequently repeated, during the first few days of the conflict. As a result, it was also reported by international news organizations, although frequently with the caveat that this was an unconfirmed figure. It never was confirmed, and every estimate of deaths since has been substantially lower. Nevertheless, Russia continued to use this figure and, in a country where the most influential media outlets rarely challenge the official line, it is probably still widely accepted. On occasions in the months following the conflict when I attempted to establish whether Russia still maintained that it was correct, I was simply told that the difficult circumstances during and following the fighting meant that the final civilian death toll had not yet been established. Human Rights Watch concluded, in a report into the conflict published in January 2009, 'To date, neither Russian nor South Ossetian officials have made clear how these figures were compiled, and what evidence supports them' (2009: 74) [17]

To Russian audiences at least, it mattered little. Whoever had thought up the figures had got their message across. The fact that these numbers, even assuming that 2,000 could have been correct, were tiny compared to the number of civilians killed by Russian forces not so far away in Chechnya in the 1990s was also ignored by the Russian media.

What both armies of PR warriors did achieve in that conflict was getting their message across. Neither agency was willing to claim victory – arguably, both wound up losing. Russia continued to be seen as irrational, unpredictable and violent. Georgia's image shifted from that of plucky little outpost of democracy to rather unstable and unreliable[18] – but then, to claim victory in the PR war would itself have seemed like clumsy public relations, as sources close to both teams privately conceded.

Still, the conflict was covered, unlike many others which fail to grab the attention of the news media. The substantial sums paid to the PR firms were part of the reason for this, but politics and technology also played an important role. Without them, the public relations armies would have had no field to fight on.

So why is it that some conflicts gain more coverage than others? What is it that drives news organizations' agendas? The straightforward answer to this is, as I suggest above, politics and technology. Two conflicts I reported on at length in the 1990s and in the first decade of the new century were Russia's wars in Chechnya, and the Israeli–Palestinian conflict. The latter received far more international media attention than the former, although the former was extensively covered at the height of Russia's second major campaign in its rebellious southern territory in the autumn and early winter of 1999.

News values and the conflicts in Chechnya and Gaza

The war in Chechnya was difficult to cover. Western journalists had been all but absent from the North Caucasus since the middle years of the 1990s because of the threat of kidnapping. Some hostages had been beheaded by their captors. The Russian military – angered and frustrated by the negative image that emerged of them from the earlier fighting in 1994–5 – did all they could to prevent foreign journalists from entering Chechnya. Those substantial obstacles of security and access limited journalists' ability to work. There were other, technical factors too. It was very difficult to send material from the region, especially if you decided to embark on something other than the usual daily news-gathering (for some weeks, this was largely limited to conversations with people fleeing from Chechnya into Ingushetia, where most of the international media were based). Venturing into unpredictable areas meant taking the risk that you would not be able to return to despatch your report in time to meet daily deadlines. And there were political issues influencing coverage, too. As with the earlier war, in 1994–5, the Russian advance caused extensive civilian casualties. When this fighting and killing were at their peak, the conflict did dominate international news bulletins. What was absent, though, was the expectation that there would be any kind of international action to try to bring the bloodshed to an end. Despite the pleas and suggestions of human rights organizations, there was never any prospect that the west was likely to try to get involved. No journalist had any illusion that their reporting might help to prompt an intervention. Britain and the United States were keen supporters of the then Russian president, Boris Yeltsin, in whom they saw a guarantor against the return of Soviet Communism, and with it, a new Cold War. Their response to Chechnya was never going to amount to anything more than verbal protest. It was hard to see what the United Nations could have done, either – even supposing it was minded to intervene. Russia was, and is, a permanent member of the Security Council. So the news agenda collided with *realpolitik*, and, after the horror and excitement expressed over the early stages of the fighting, Chechnya dropped off the editorial radar. The conflict is referred to when, as in March 2010 on the Moscow metro, Chechens carry out deadly attacks on Russian civilian targets. A reflection of how poorly the detail of the situation there is understood, even among some otherwise learned observers, can be found in the fact that Tumber and Webster refer to Russian troops in Chechnya, operating within the borders of the Russian Federation, as 'occupiers' (2006: 37).

The Israeli–Palestinian conflict is different. In this case, Israel's advanced infrastructure means that technology is readily accessible to international journalists working there. The ease with which material can be sent from Israel definitely contributes to the extensive coverage that that conflict receives at times of fighting, or heightened tension. Arguably, the fact that Israel's infrastructure is superior to that of the Palestinian territories means that its opinions are more widely broadcast. When I was the BBC correspondent in Gaza, producers in London would sometimes decide to take a report from one of my colleagues in Jerusalem, even if the story was in Gaza, because my colleague there could more easily appear 'in vision'. Of course, this is not the only reason offered to explain Israel's success in getting its opinions heard. As Philo *et al.* write, 'This is in part a result of the success of the public relations initiatives undertaken by Israel, and the superior quality of their "news machine"' (2003: 148).

Naturally, politics too helps this conflict to prominence on the international news agenda. The idea that a peace deal between Israel and the Palestinians, and the creation of a Palestinian state, would improve relations between the west and the Arab-Muslim world is a powerful one – and successive presidents of the United States have striven to bring this about. The amount of Washington's diplomatic time spent in arranging and hosting talks to try to get the two sides to agree means that this is a conflict that receives extensive coverage – no matter that the extent of the killing and destruction of property there is dwarfed by that which has happened in recent years in Chechnya, Darfur or the Democratic Republic of Congo. Political and diplomatic forces are not the only ones here – Paul Moorcraft and Philip Taylor suggest that 'famine-like conditions and the intimidating tribal complexities' were part of the reason why 'so few journalists spent long enough in the country to get a handle on the story' (2008: 206) of Darfur – but they are the most influential. As Susan Sontag wrote, when considering the amount of media attention given to the Israeli–Palestinian conflict,

> In the meantime, far crueler wars in which civilians are relentlessly slaughtered from the air and massacred on the ground (the decades-long civil war in Sudan, the Iraqi campaigns against the Kurds, the Russian invasions and occupation of Chechnya) have gone relatively unphotographed.[19]
>
> (2003: 33)

News values, in other words, are largely dictated by the importance that political elites place upon different conflicts. I said in Chapter 1 that my definition of politics as a factor in conflict reporting is the broadest one possible – so here I would like to mention another issue which I believe falls under that. Prasun Sonwalkar persuasively makes the case that 'journalists are invariably drawn from the "national main-stream" and circularly cater to this section of society and its value system' (2004: 208). Although his study is largely limited to India, his conclusions have a much wider relevance.

A few days after the attacks of September 11, I saw a cartoon in a newspaper I bought in New York State on my way to Manhattan. In the picture, a typical American family ignore the television screen which shows the twin towers in flames. Instead, they are reading magazines about sport and celebrity culture, and wondering aloud who their enemies might be. They have no idea. The cartoon seems to echo Sonwalkar's warning that 'In an age of globalization of terror, such selectivity of news reporting can have serious implications' (ibid.: 201).

Conclusion: the threats Conflict News Management poses to audiences' understanding

Sonwalkar's argument heralds a wider debate about how we should cover conflict today. I interpret the second extract quoted above as his attempt to make the case for a changed world to have changed editorial priorities. I will return to this in the final chapter: the points he addresses are ones that I believe demand urgent attention, and a break with past convention. Other methods that the meticulous reporter can and should employ to repel the PR pirates rely on a thorough applica-tion of long-established good practice: try to stick with what you know to be true, or reliably reported. I remember having a long discussion with a colleague about whether you should report something just because a prominent person says it. I maintained that the journalist's duty, especially as a foreign correspondent, is to use their experience and knowledge to weigh up a statement and put it in context, rather than simply relaying it. That latter task, after all, is the job of a spokesperson. If you suspect you are being deliberately misled, say so, or don't even bother to report what you can reasonably conclude is propaganda. Scary whispers from 'security sources' often fall into this category.

A strong news story shares many characteristics with a good piece of fiction. Aside from the fact that one is supposed to be true, and the other not, both need a storyline, characters and dramatic events to draw in and fascinate the audience. Those elements are often present in war, one of the most extreme of human experiences. Journalists reporting conflict must remember that public relations agents, and government spin doctors, are very well aware of this, and that reporters are desperate for anything that will make their story distinctive or strong. In wartime especially, news organizations must not allow mercenary consultancies to occupy their territory. Should they do this, they will find that their audiences' understanding will be the real casualty: invaded by waves of propaganda, and cut off from truth. The idea of the CNN effect – the suggestion that government policy can be quickly influenced by the impact of news reporting – is long established, even if the scholar who first named it as such, Piers Robinson, later concluded 'subsequent research has demonstrated that the CNN effect was largely exaggerated' (2004: 108). What might be called the CNM – 'Conflict News Management' – effect is not exaggerated, and is a growing threat to our understanding as citizens, of wars which are waged in our name.

Summary

- the importance that belligerents in contemporary conflicts place on fighting, and winning, the public relations war.
- Russia and Georgia's evolving use of tactics and resources during their 2008 war over South Ossetia
- the wider implications of the attempts of governments and their advisors to influence journalism in wartime
- news values and Chechnya and Gaza
- the CNM (Conflict News Management) effect

5 Multi-platform storytelling

'There's no way that I can think of myself as a war correspondent without stopping to acknowledge the degree to which it's pure affectation,' writes Michael Herr in *Dispatches*. 'I never had to run back to any bureau or office to file,' he reflects, noting the more leisurely deadlines that came with his work for a magazine (1977: 171). Today, he would probably be blogging, or tweeting or both, whoever he was working for. Changes in technology over the decades since Herr covered the Vietnam War have been both a boon and a burden to all journalists. For those working in conflict zones, the combined advantage and disadvantage is especially acute.

Some recent studies of news media and technology

Any analysis of journalism and new technology is inevitably difficult due to the accelerated pace of change, rendering anything written now out of date within a couple of years. Tumber and Webster (2006: 82) include a section on the way that 'new technologies' are affecting 'frontline journalism' but their reference to use of the internet as a research tool as a 'recent' development seems to illustrate the problem. Studies of journalism and technology have tended to focus on the effect that technological change has on the way that news is presented: specifically, on whether new technology is creating new journalism, or whether it is a case of the same game between media and governments being played with different equipment. As Robinson *et al.* summarize it,

> Many academics and commentators argue that the ending of the cold war and the expansion of communications technology have extended the scope for more independent and critical news media. Conversely, some argue that strengthened media-management operations have ensured a continued advantage for governments pursuing war.
>
> (2010: 25)

In *The Al Jazeera Effect: How the New Global Media Are Reshaping World Politics*, Philip Seib states that 'the expanded array of news providers alters political dynamics throughout the world. Policymakers are, however slowly, recognizing this' (2008: 45). Those writers who are more cautious, or even cynical, about the benefits that technological change can bring, might add that policy-makers are recognizing the potential that social networking presents for keeping an eye on people. As Evgeny Morozov notes in *Net Delusion: The Dark Side of Internet Freedom*, in a chapter provocatively entitled 'Why the KGB Wants You to Join Facebook',

> Your security is only as good as that of the computer you are working on; the more people have access to it, the more likely it is that someone could turn your computer into a spying machine. Given that a lot of internet activism takes place on public computers, security compromises abound
>
> (2011: 170)

Susan Carruthers makes the interesting, related point that the proliferation of social media has affected the way that armies have to look at private communication,

> For young servicemen and women who'd grown up in the Web 2.0 age, formal oversight of private communications seemed almost impossible to conceive. Meanwhile, for officers too old to have grown up with instant-messaging and Facebook, clamping down on social media appeared almost as difficult to execute – as unpopular an expedient as it was technically challenging.
>
> (2011: 245)

This idea of 'formal oversight of private communications' is a very important one, to which I will return in Chapter 7, in looking at how both Israel and Hamas have tried to use social media both for attack and defence. While the extracts above reflect the differing views of whether or not new technology is good news for journalism, there seems little dispute that it is changing it – and no reporter would disagree. In *Supermedia*, Charlie Beckett offers a useful and well-observed summary of how he sees the dilemma facing reporting. 'If it is to have any value then journalism must retain its core ethics and vital skills. But if it is to survive then it must adapt. It must go further than that and offer something more' (2008: 41). Beckett's words now read like an accurate prediction of the debate that new media have provoked in news organizations: how to get the best out of the traditional journalist's craft in a time when the media themselves are evolving.

So writers of recent years have looked at new technology as it affects relations between the media and the state; its effects on policy; its potential as a tool of suppression rather than liberation (at the time of writing, some anecdotal evidence suggests that the Syrian secret police are using social media to monitor activists campaigning against the continuing rule of President Bashar al-Assad); and the challenges it presents to conventional journalism. What I feel has been less well documented – although Tumber and Webster (2006: 82) do write about it – is the effect of new technology on the newsgathering process.

New technology and the newsgathering process: the 'Arab spring' of 2011

Advances in technology may have made the conflict reporter's job simpler in some senses – it is easier than ever to send material, and to stay in touch with colleagues – but they have complicated it in others. Digital technology has also brought one important advance that represents an unprecedented change in the way in which news is gathered: user-generated content. A definition of UGC a few years ago might have read like an updated version of 'amateur video' – pictures, often exclusive ones of an event actually happening – sent in by amateurs after they managed by luck or judgement to capture what the professionals missed. Now, especially after the protests that followed Iran's election in 2009, and the uprisings in North Africa and the Middle East in the spring of 2011, social networking sites, particularly Twitter and Facebook, must also be taken into account.

One established view of the effect of UGC holds that the spread of digital technology means that tyrants and war criminals will find it harder and harder to silence the message of those who seek to expose wrongdoing. With so many committed citizens now able to video material on their phones and upload it to the internet, or even just send text messages (Seib, 2008: 114), the true story will out, whether or not this or that oppressive regime wants it. There is undoubtedly some truth to this. Video pictures can be captured and distributed with an ease that would have seemed the stuff of science fiction not too long ago. This material often has great impact. Think, for example, of the *Guardian*'s reports on the death of Ian Tomlinson during the G20 protests in

London in 2009 (Pearse and Weaver, 2009). Even if it was old technology, in the form of a printed newspaper, which gave the story its initial prominence, the coverage as a whole was shaped by the digital-age phenomena of mobile-phone footage, and the broadcasting of this on the *Guardian* website.

Media reports of the protests and uprisings that spread across North Africa and the Middle East in the spring of 2011 made frequent reference to activists' use of social-networking sites. A blog entry on the website of the *Washington Post*, 'Egypt protests "Day of Departure" Day 11' included pictures from Cairo showing signs and graffiti apparently thanking Facebook and Twitter (Bell, 2011). At the time of writing, it is not possible to determine definitively the effect that social media may or may not have had in the process that drove President Hosni Mubarak from power. The protests, after all, were prompted by poor economic conditions and opposition to the conduct of the Egyptian security forces – not by the existence of Facebook or Twitter. Users of social media in the protests in Syria were not able to succeed in their aims as their counterparts in Egypt did, and there were some high-profile reminders of both the potential fallibility of sources which are impossible to verify, and the real limits of social media. The *Guardian* and other news media were taken in by a blog purporting to be the work of a Syrian lesbian and activist, Amina Arraf, but which was in fact the work of an American man (McCrum, 2011). In June 2011, Reuters described the organizational challenges faced by anti-Gaddafi protesters once the government closed off internet access (Al-Khairalla and Carey, 2011).

The protests were the making of a new medium for reporting news, and proof of the continuing influence of an older one. 'Live blogging' – a minute-by-minute news report on a website – arguably came of age as a news medium during the protests (although the form had existed for years for sport). Matt Wells wrote in the *Guardian* in March 2011, 'as the Arab revolutions have unfolded, live blogging has rapidly become the dominant form for breaking news online' (Wells, 2011). The great advantage of the live blog is the ability to assimilate material from professional and audience sources in order to get the best of both. The 'Arab spring' was also a moment of triumph for Al-Jazeera English, whose coverage of the uprisings led to complimentary profiles in other news media (Plunkett and Halliday, 2011; Arlidge, 2011). While Al-Jazeera's website (along with those of the BBC, the *Guardian* and other news organizations) did feature live blogs, the channel's reputation was enhanced not because of technical innovation, but because of its content: its ability to make good use of the resources it had in the region. In that sense, Al-Jazeera's success in the spring of 2011 confirmed the enduring influence of a medium from the pre-Twitter age: satellite TV news channels.

Rooftop journalism: repeating the news rather than reporting it?

They had been around since the 1990s, increasingly employing the live, round-the-clock format which has been so widely reproduced (Thussu, 2003: 117). One of the biggest challenges for today's reporter in conflict zones, as elsewhere, is time management. 'Rooftop journalism' – as hourly live reporting from the nearest place to a war affording a reliable power supply good communications and preferably a panoramic view more or less related to the story is known – has cut into time which might once have been spent collecting material. Especially in a time of tighter budgets, news organizations want to get plenty of airtime and newspaper pages filled in return for the expense of a costly deployment. On a big story, large companies like the BBC will often deploy a reporter whose main role is to provide live report after live report for the corporation's twenty-four-hour news channels. This was a role I had in Basra in 2004, part of the coverage of the first anniversary of the invasion of Iraq. On that occasion, because it was a planned event, I was able to spend a couple of days in the area trying to get a sense of what was happening, so that I could talk with at least some authority in the many live broadcasts which followed. It is not always the way. Early on in the era of continuous news channels, Martin Bell pointed out the disadvantages in what he saw:

> There were days in Sarajevo when my radio colleague, who was already working for a rolling news service, had to broadcast as many as twenty-eight separate reports. Not only did he never leave the Holiday Inn, he hardly had time to pick up the phone and talk to the UN spokesman.
>
> (1995: 28–9)

Since Martin Bell was writing in the 1990s, that situation has only become more common. The trend has accelerated. Within the BBC, an additional factor is that the reporter doing all those live radio or TV reports may be the junior member of the team: the one who is most likely to be paid per piece that they file. So they actually have a financial incentive to satisfy the constant demand from London for live updates, whether or not there is actually anything new to say. The financial incentive may be especially strong if that stringer (as a freelance, or sponsored, rather than staff, reporter is usually called) has had a lean time of it in the time preceding that particular story. That is often the case in less frequently covered parts of the globe where, to a mainstream news audience, conflict can seem to flare up as if from nothing. The disadvantage of all this is exactly as Bell describes: the reporter does not have the time to pick up the phone to a UN spokesman, or anyone else.

The shortcomings and weaknesses of this kind of 'rooftop journalism' have been extensively discussed (Paterson and Sreberny, 2004: 6; Tumber and Webster 2006: 93–4). In my last years at the BBC, during my posting to Moscow from 2006–9, senior editors were wise enough to address the matter. The result was that a number of 'windows' – certain times during the day – were identified. During these slots, programmes could ask for a live report. At other times, correspondents were expected to go live only when they actually had something new to report.

What has been discussed less – and this seems to me to be no less an issue – is the demand that multimedia newsgathering places on a reporter's time. Most journalists keep the time they spend in areas where fighting is happening, or could start at any moment, as short as possible. In the last chapter, I looked at attempts to influence reporting which begin far from the front line. Now I would like to look at challenges which emerge on the front line.

Like any journalist working to tight deadlines, the reporter in a conflict zone has to cope with the pressures of time, and conflicting demands. The journalist covering war can often add to those pressures physical danger, being outside for long periods in extreme cold or heat, limited supplies of food and water. But the harshest of those pressures can be the ones held in common with any other reporter up against the clock on a big story: using time as efficiently as possible. Here, though, there are two big differences: danger, and deadly consequences. Staying in the wrong place for too long can put the reporter, or their colleagues, at great risk. Making a mistake in a report from such a place could lead to much worse than an irate phone call from a minister's spin doctor, or a celebrity's PR advisor. It could lead to a death threat, or, in extreme cases, an upsurge in fighting.

Newsgathering for multiple platforms: Case study 1, reporting from Rafah

Rafah, at the southern end of the Gaza Strip where that territory borders Egypt, was especially dangerous during the *intifada* from 2000 onwards, and became so again during Israel's massive military operation in Gaza in early 2009. When I was based in Gaza from 2002–4, the Israelis cleared an area between the edge of the refugee camp (a shanty town that shared the name of the place next to which it had grown up) and their military post, which lay on the border with Egypt. Clearing the area – which they did so that they could see anyone approaching the huge metal fence which they had built to protect their position – meant demolishing countless houses, which they said had been used by Palestinian fighters as firing positions.

The houses were generally demolished at night. I decided against trying to report on this as it happened. Filming in Rafah at night seemed simply too dangerous. The cameraman with whom I usually worked at the time, Ian Druce, agreed with this decision. Our judgement was proved shockingly correct when, in May 2003, Israeli soldiers shot and killed James Miller, a documentary director and cameraman, while he was filming there during the hours of darkness.

We had to do the story, though. It could not be ignored. It was an important part of the conflict for, as well as destroying houses which they alleged were used by militants, the Israelis also blew up the homes of people they suspected of carrying out attacks on Israeli targets. The edge of Rafah refugee camp was normally deserted. The alleys which led towards the open ground were so narrow you could touch the walls of the houses on either side with your outstretched arms, and even the midday Middle Eastern sun seemed barely to reach there. In other places, there were broader streets, their ends blocked off by mounds of earth designed to protect pedestrians, and to impede the progress of armoured vehicles when they sought to enter. It was not a place to linger.

My colleagues and I would take some pictures, film an interview or two with people who lived there, and whose houses were under threat of demolition, film a piece to camera, record some on-location radio links, and leave. Yet there was always pressure to record a longer, or different, additional piece to camera for another programme; take some pictures for the website; record an entire radio news report there and then. Sometimes these extra items were possible, sometimes not. Increasingly, they are seen as an indispensable part of any such trip to gather material. That leaves the reporter with a series of difficult choices as he or she decides what to prioritize. Do all the different versions of the same recording, and forget the interview which might give you the best description of what happens there? Or get the interview, and endure the complaints of the editor who had not got exactly what he or she wanted, even if the other programmes and platforms were satisfied? Few reporters come away from a place like that feeling content that they have managed to tell the story to everyone who needs to know it. I think it is true to say that, while in recent years many journalists have found the demand to do extra versions burdensome, they do understand that it is necessary. Television news may have retained its dominance as a news medium in a way that many predicted it would not – AJE's success is an example of that – but dominance does not mean exclusivity. Our audiences expect to find us on different platforms, and we have to satisfy that expectation – which can often be intensified in time of war. The days of sending a single report for a single medium – as Michael Herr did – are all but over. Reporters today have to accept that, even as so doing involves accepting a system that limits your time to gather facts.

A reporter's sense of self-worth, and their job satisfaction, are not the only casualties of this. The time-consuming nature of multimedia newsgathering is mirrored in the time taken up in editing at least three separate versions of the same piece for different platforms. Because, in the case of an 'on-the-day' news story, when all of them are hugely time-sensitive, the different versions must be put together as quickly as circumstances allow. When I say 'at least' three versions, I mean television, radio and online. In addition to all this, reporters are increasingly tweeting too. Each medium may itself actually require more than one version. Online, for example, may merit a text piece with some illustration, and if the story is an especially strong one pictorially (obviously, this is often the case in a war zone), then there may be a picture gallery to prepare too. TV and the web can overlap, with requests for long pieces to camera – known in the BBC as 'rants' – in which the reporter walks through a location describing what has happened there, or explaining what the audience can see around him or her. As well as being posted on the website, these rants may also be broadcast on the BBC News channel, or BBC World News. Sometimes, the reporter will be asked to record a rant in advance of an event – something which, with the addition of part of the word 'speculate', I came to call a 'specurant'. There may be different versions for international and domestic platforms. And the team members who have gathered the material – typically, at the BBC, a team of correspondent, producer and shoot-edit (that is, camera operator and picture editor) – will have to decide how they will put these divergent versions together. Naturally, the shoot-edit will be mainly involved with the TV version rather than those for radio or online.

How does this all work in practice, especially in areas where infrastructure is often wrecked, or was never that good in the first place? It is rare now to be in an area where there is absolutely no mobile-phone coverage, but it does happen. In 2008, there was only one Russian mobile-phone operator whose SIM cards worked in Chechnya. For those of us who weren't subscribers to that network, that meant changing over to another card on arrival in the region (and cutting yourself off from anyone who might be trying to contact you on your customary number). Still, that was not an insurmountable difficulty. What is harder is when travel to the area where the news is takes hours in itself – and the return journey is eating into your airtime. This is particularly true when you are working for a continuous news network, which, by definition, has no fixed deadlines. 'They want it yesterday' is a frequent intake editor's response to a correspondent asking how long he has got.

Case study 2: South Ossetia

In October 2008, I travelled to North Ossetia (part of the Russian Federation) to join a Russian Army press trip into South Ossetia (part of Georgia which, following a brief war in August that year, Russia had recognized as an independent state). Mobile-phone coverage in North Ossetia was mostly pretty good: on the drive from the airport to the town of Vladikavkaz, I was able to read which opponents the football team I supported would face in that season's UEFA Cup.

We left before dawn the next morning to travel through the Roki tunnel, a feat of Soviet-era engineering which bored a hole through the Caucasus Mountains. It was the route taken by the Russian forces who had poured into South Ossetia in support of the separatists some two months earlier. Our eventual destination, after stopping at a Russian Army base inside the disputed territory to change vehicles, was Karaleti, a village near which the Russians were dismantling a post they had set up in the aftermath of their invasion. The intention was to show the press that they were complying with the terms of the truce. The village lay beyond the administrative border of South Ossetia, in undisputed Georgian territory. We were moved into an armoured truck ostensibly for our own safety, although it was hard to escape the conclusion that the real motive was to prevent our seeing the amount of Georgian civilian property which the Russians and their South Ossetian irregular allies had destroyed. The view from inside the armoured truck was very restricted. There were no windows in the sides, so we could see only what we had just passed as it became more distant.

The drive to Karaleti took around six hours. We were then permitted to see the Russians making the final preparations for their departure; interview a senior officer; and film the column heading north while European Union monitors looked on (Rodgers, 2008b). The whole time we were working amounted to around an hour and a half. We then had to begin the long journey back – time given as the reason for denying us the chance to seek out our South Ossetian hosts from a trip made a couple of years earlier. It was deeply frustrating.

Still, despite the paucity of material, we did actually have a story. On the bumpy bus ride back up the southern slopes of the Caucasus, I began to scribble down in my notebook a story for the website. I filed it by telephone at the top of the mountain pass – grateful still to the patient colleague in London who later transcribed it (Rodgers, 2008a). Worried in advance that we would be short of time, we had arranged for a driver to come to meet us at the pass (the furthest a civilian vehicle was allowed to travel – the tunnel was off limits then to those without permission) to take us back to our hotel more quickly. That was the first place from which we would actually be able to send our TV report. While we drove, the shoot-edit, Anton Chicherov, looked through the pictures on a laptop. I discussed structure with him and our producer, Daria Merkusheva. Once we were back, we put the piece together as rapidly as possible – striving to keep it simple, and to make the most of the very short time we had actually spent filming. We knew that sending our material to London, via an unreliable internet connection, would take an age – and with every minute, our report was getting older. As Anton and I finished the TV version, Daria prepared the interview clips and sound for a radio news report – a 'long' version of around three and a half minutes, and a shorter one.

Even with as straightforward a story as this, 'the Russians have removed a military post from an area of Georgia which they occupied in August', the task of editing involved challenges and complexities. The editorial process for each medium is different. If the opening shot for the TV package is stunning visually, and yet has no sound, then the audio equivalent will not work for radio. A fleeting impression – carefully described in a script – of a burnt-out building glimpsed from the armoured truck might have worked well for radio. It could have been the start of a link about civilian deaths and damage to property but, if the camera was not running on the ruin the reporter had in mind, it would not work for TV. And the striking words of a soldier or refugee might make a strong start to text for the web, but it would not work as the opening to a conventional broadcast news report, either for radio or television. All this structuring and restructuring can be extremely time-consuming and, if the decisions are not obvious ones, the reporter can continue to ask him or herself questions about whether the right ones were taken long after the material is broadcast or published. On that occasion, we finished sending our material, and ate our first meal of the day, at almost midnight – nearly twenty hours after we had got up for our pre-dawn departure.

Of course, the frustration was more than compensated for by the satisfaction that we had actually managed to file for all three platforms, and by fascination at what we had seen. Once a reporter ceases to be interested in what he or she sees, despite hunger or other temporary hardship, then they should no longer be doing the job. I was pleased to have been able to return to the place I had last visited before the conflict, even if the view which my trip afforded me was literally blinkered. I felt that was a piece of the puzzle which made my view of the conflict at least a little more complete (this was a couple of weeks before I went to interview the public relations consultants who had sought to direct the story of the war from their comfortable offices in Brussels). But my time to compose my thoughts had been short to begin with, and shortened still further by the need to edit more than one version. I stress again that I understand why, and felt as great a duty to my audience on all platforms – but it was not ideal.

The expectation that a correspondent will furnish material for multiple platforms, combined with the recent realities of newsgathering (where even big, established and relatively well-resourced media organizations will have fewer permanent overseas bureaux) are putting extra pressures on a job which has always been one where time was tight. As Tumber and Webster note,

> Frontline correspondents work on short notice of assignments, making it difficult for them to be informed about every country. Research time is often very limited. Journalists can be told to get on a plane straight away to cover a conflict or disaster. With the spread of presenter/journalists reporting live from location rather than the studio this may be happening more frequently.

(2006: 77)

The despatching of senior presenters to cover major stories is not a completely new trend – foreign-correspondent folklore has its store of tales of household names sent out at short notice, and struggling to pronounce key names with which the local press corps is comfortably familiar – but it is becoming more common. At their best, deployments of this sort allow experienced and high-profile reporters to bring their skills to a complex but important story, the significance of which an unfamiliar audience may not immediately see. At their worst, they lead international newsgathering – and here I am thinking in particular of television coverage – into a rigid set of templates where every conflict has a goody a baddy and some innocent victims, preferably orphans, paying the price.

This formulaic package-making is the enemy of understanding. Lord Copper, Evelyn Waugh's caricature of a 1930s press baron in *Scoop* may have been a comic creation, but, like so many of the elements of that stinging satire, he stood for a deeper truth about the business of news both then, and now. Lord Copper announces the policy of his newspaper, *The Beast* for the war in Africa which his correspondent is about to leave to cover:

> The British public has no interest in a war which drags on indecisively. A few sharp victories, some conspicuous acts of personal bravery on the patriot side, and a colourful entry into the capital. That is *The Beast* policy for the war.
>
> (1938: 42)

That kind of attitude is still commonplace today. Studying the coverage of the 2003 invasion of Iraq, Robinson *et al.* describe 'stories of British raids written up in the heroic language of boys-own fiction' (2010: 86). Huge assumptions are sometimes made on behalf of the audience about what might interest them.[20] Overemphasis on human interest angles in war zones, as a means of telling a story in a way which will have the greatest impact, can sometimes lead to oversimplification. Lord Copper would surely recognize his 'conspicuous acts of personal bravery on the patriot side' today. Their contemporary equivalent is easily found. Formulaic package-making is the result of the reluctant admission on the part of a news organization that a particular conflict has become newsworthy to the extent that it cannot be ignored. That acceptance may lead to their sending a star 'special correspondent' to report on it. Especially in the era of multi-platform news, and squeezed budgets, that correspondent will be under pressure to deliver and, as always, to outshine any competitors.

That is when they may have to fall back on the formula. The formula will usually involve identifying one side as 'victims of terrorist atrocities', or 'victims of massacres'. These roles may already have been established in the accepted – i.e. western – understanding of the conflict, and it is not the formulaic correspondent's job to challenge that, so much as to confirm it. In such cases, it is hard not to agree with Jean Seaton's suggestion that, 'the pressure to fit events into well understood frameworks is intense' (2003: 51). Alternatively, there may not always be obvious 'goodies', (Lord Copper's 'patriot side') and baddies, so the poorly briefed correspondent can always fall back on the approach that each belligerent is as bad as the other. Then they need to identify the victims to bring their story to life – a trip to an orphanage or an old people's home often does the trick. To be clear: reporting on orphanages, hospitals and old people's homes is often the best way of explaining human suffering in conflict. It is not, in itself, without context, a means of explaining to audiences what they are seeing. The real danger from formulaic package-making is that it reinforces images of suffering in some parts of the world to the extent that audiences come to believe that that is the normal state of affairs; that conflict in place X or Y is just the sort of thing that happens there, and there is not very much we can do about it.

Susan Carruthers has summarized this effect succinctly:

> As frequently represented, atavistic bloodletting lacks rational explanation but perpetually simmers, occasionally boiling over, in the 'Balkans' or 'darkest' Africa. Besides removing any further obligation to understand the roots of conflict, explaining violence as inexplicable may also be conveniently self serving: if ethnic violence is age-old and engrained, then there is little that onlooking states or international organisations can do.
>
> (2000: 44–5)

Carruthers (2011: 5) and Jean Seaton (2003: 49) have also written about war as a selling point for news. We are used to hearing that newspaper circulations have soared, or ratings figures for broadcast news programmes jumped dramatically, in time of war but, as she points out, this is not a new phenomenon for the digital age. The thirst for news in wartime, and the resultant increase in sales, is as old as the mass media themselves (remember John Reed's witnessing the crowds in revolutionary St Petersburg fighting over the 'feverish little sheet of four pages, containing no news'(1977: 95–6)). This demand can also be a driving factor towards formulaic reporting. Elements of a story which might complicate its easy communication may be omitted, whether or not they are significant. The formulaic report can feel like a frustrating page on a website where one must leave information. There are certain fields with red asterisks which demand to be completed. There may or may not be a field for other relevant facts or explanations.

Does new technology – with its advantages and disadvantages – offer the opportunity to improve this? I examine that question in detail in my concluding chapter. In the next chapter, I look at the lessons for conflict reporting that can be drawn from the coverage of Israel's military operation in Gaza in January 2009. Before that I would like to consider that assault, known as 'Operation Cast Lead', as an example of the use of UGC in covering war.

UGC in war reporting, and its limits: Gaza 2009

In the last week of December 2008, Israel launched 'Operation Cast Lead', a massive assault on the Gaza Strip. The publicly stated aim of the offensive was to put an end to the firing of rockets from inside the territory at targets in the adjacent south of Israel. The result was a massive loss of Palestinian life: 1,400, according to Palestinian sources, although the Israelis put the figure at the slightly lower 1,166 (BBC World Service, 2010). The number of those killed who were combatants rather than civilians is likewise the subject of disagreement – but that there were a large number of civilian deaths is beyond dispute. There were also reports which came to light in the weeks after the assault, based on Israeli sources, which suggested that Israeli troops had deliberately targeted Palestinian civilians (BBC News, 2009). Allegations of this nature are not new to Palestinians. Their experience of the Israeli Army would lead them to believe such reports without question. They were newsworthy at the time for the way that they appeared to confirm suspicions that part of the Israeli Army's purpose in conducting the operation in the way that it did was to hit the Palestinians so hard that they would think twice before launching any further attacks on Israel. In this, 'Cast Lead' was only partially successful, as the BBC's Middle East correspondent, Paul Wood, noted in his analysis some two months after the offensive (Wood, 2009).

With most international news organizations kept away – Al-Jazeera, which already had a correspondent inside Gaza was an exception – reporting responsibilities fell to Palestinian journalists, and non-journalists.

Video captured on mobile phones found its way to the outside world via websites appealing directly for material, or via Palestinian journalists who took it upon themselves to gather it, and package it for the news organizations which employed them. There is no question that some of this material was extremely strong (there is analysis of some of the coverage in the next chapter). It did convey the complete defenceless-ness of those caught in the crossfire in that most densely populated of territories. Pictures of streets, schools, playgrounds and hospitals under fire reinforced the sense that these were the ordinary things of life visited by a war from which those wanting an ordinary life could not escape. As in other news stories of war or disaster, the shaky amateur pictures somehow make a shocking event seem more immediate; even more unexpected and, so, more horrific. There was a sense among those of us watching from outside the war zone that the story had at least come out.

Of course it had – but how completely? This was in one sense a triumph for UGC, proof that denying access to professional reporters from outside the territory would not stop the story reaching the world. It was an important moment for assessing digital technology's contribu-tion to reporting conflict. Alongside that sense of journalistic success, there is a need for sober reflection upon the limits of what UGC can actually achieve. To begin with, the sheer volume of available material means that it is difficult to view all of it. More importantly in a case like this, it makes it very difficult to verify. In the absence of one of their own journalists who can vouch for what the viewer sees, news organi-zations are taking considerable risks with their reputation for reliability. Major news organizations have made blunders in the past by showing professionally shot pictures in the wrong context. How much more likely is such an error in the case of UGC, how much more serious the consequences to journalistic credibility if such a mistake were made in such a controversial conflict? It does not even matter if the mistake is a genuine one or not. News coverage is judged in the moment – later corrections, or vindications, carry less weight. One of the weaknesses of UGC is that – because of issues outlined above – doubt can more read-ily be cast upon it. Subsequent material supporting the assertion that was originally made is bound to have less impact that that which is said and seen in the moment. Israel's image to some extent suffered from frequent on-air and published reminders that it was, in effect, censoring the news media. But Israel has endured worse press coverage, and its army probably would have done so on this occasion had the decision not been taken to keep reporters out.

What did the news executives themselves think? At the time, senior representatives of most international news organizations shared their correspondents' frustrations at being banned. A few months after the Israeli operation, I attended a private event at which senior editors from major news media discussed what the effect had been of Israel's actions. While they noted the role that UGC had played in trying to lessen the effects of the ban, they seemed reluctantly to agree that the ban had served Israel's purpose nevertheless. Syria's ban on foreign correspondents, still in force at the time of writing (June 2011) seemed to have its desired effect too. That is not to say, of course, that such a conclusion is inevitable. Israel and its armed forces expend a considerable deal of effort on polishing their international image. In Hebrew, there is a single word, 'hasbara', which is used to describe public diplomacy on Israel's behalf. Israel pays a lot of attention to the media coverage that it receives. Even if it does not allow itself to be influenced by criticism, it wants to know what that criticism says. During 'Cast Lead', it went a step further, and did its best even to manage the kind of criticism to which it could be subjected.

Conclusion: the pluses and minuses of new technology in conflict journalism

UGC might well have proved the complete undoing of a less effective military spin machine. But the obstacles in the way of good conflict reporting have only changed in the digital age; they have not disappeared, or dissolved. Widespread digital technology has found more holes in the fences which are placed in the way of reporters, but it has not made the walls come tumbling down. In this respect, I would argue that Seib (2008: 45) and Robinson *et al.* (2010: 25) are right to highlight the dual nature of technological change: it is not a story of progress alone. New technology will not guarantee a diminution of political influence. In one important sense, it has placed extra responsibilities on the shoulders of journalists covering conflict. The material you send can now be seen much more widely than ever before. Your report may be available on the internet to the people who feature in it, and their enemies. Tumber and Webster raise the issue of 'pressure and threats that come from groups who find what has been reported about them to be disagreeable' (2006: 83), and they are right to do so. In Iraq in 2003, I did a live broadcast from a village north of Baghdad. Just as I started to speak, the street emptied. Many of the curious bystanders had rushed into the village tea shop, apparently to watch the television there, and check our claim that we were going to be on the BBC. They were satisfied that we had been telling the truth, and it demonstrated to me and my colleagues how close we could now be to audiences in apparently remote and underdeveloped areas. The greater availability of mobile phones with internet access has only increased that closeness.

In the extract at the beginning of this chapter, Michael Herr is honest enough to admit that his was not the typical experience of a reporter in Vietnam. You can sense his relief when he relates that his work spared him the dull round of events, such as the visits of officials from the US or from third countries, which so many of his fellow journalists were forced to attend. Perhaps because of that, he has left us the most enduring account of what it was like to cover the war, an account that still aids our understanding of what happened. For Herr's ability to take the eternal from the transitory, as Charles Baudelaire said in his essay 'The Painter of Modern Life' (1968: 553), means that his account of covering a war in the 1960s is still widely read and admired in this new century. Summarizing his experience towards the end of the book, Herr concludes, 'Conventional journalism could no more reveal this war than conventional firepower could win it' (1977: 175).

In an era when we fret over the failure of 'conventional journalism' to expose the weaknesses, such as the lack of weapons of mass destruction, in the case made by the US and UK governments for invading Iraq; when that same 'conventional journalism' was seduced into overplaying the significance of the capture of Saddam Hussein, even as the biggest challenge for the occupiers of Iraq was about to begin, in the shape of the insurgency which followed a few months later; when 'conventional journalism', either through knavery or foolishness, left the looming global financial crisis of 2008 largely unreported, the clarity and meaning of Herr's words are undiminished by the intervening years. If his analysis and opinions have endured though, much about Herr's – admittedly atypical – experience, and that of his contemporaries, has changed. Herr tells the story of a colleague apologetically turning down his offer of a drink because he has to file, something which, unlike Herr, he has to do 'every day'. Today's reporters have to file several times a day, in many cases, for different platforms. To the frustration of those of us who, like Michael Herr's contemporaries, work in daily news, the most memorable accounts are often compiled some time afterwards – the enduring influence and relevance of *Dispatches* are surely proof of this – but neither daily paper nor podcast was ever able to wait for those.

Summary

- changing technology a boon and a burden to journalists
- social media, live blogging and the 'Arab spring'
- the drawbacks of 'rooftop journalism'
- multimedia newsgathering
- case studies of Rafah and South Ossetia
- UGC and the reporting of Israel's assault on Gaza in January 2009

6 'Remember it's not your war': reporter involvement

'You mean you don't have to be here?' asked the taller of the two sentries.

'No,' I answered.

'What did you think? That journalists just sit around on the sofa all day?' a Russian colleague asked the soldier.

'No. They drink coffee too,' he replied, with a mixture of scornful disbelief and disgust.

The Russian reporter and I had got talking to a pair of soldiers guarding one of the entrances to the Russian military base at Mozdok, in the North Caucasus, in March 2000. The fiercest phase of the second Chechen war was coming to an end. It was just before an election which confirmed Vladimir Putin, then Russia's acting president, in his post. It had never occurred to me that soldiers might not realize that I was covering the war through choice. The fact that they were forced to be there made it logical enough for them to believe that anyone else they met had also been constrained to come. In *Dispatches*, Michael Herr has a similar experience:

> 'Lemmee ... lemmee jus' hang on that a minute,' he said. 'You mean you don' *have* to be here? An' you're *here*?'
>
> I nodded.
>
> 'Well, they gotta be payin' you some tough bread.' (1977: 99)

At the end of *Dispatches*, when he considers what it is like to be away from the war zone, Herr says that he and his contemporaries left Vietnam because 'we all knew that if you stayed too long you became one of those poor bastards who had to have a war on all the time, and where was that' (ibid.: 195)?

There are any number of motives that draw reporters to cover war: a desire for adventure, a sense of duty, patriotism, the hope of career advancement or the opportunity to escape from something else – akin to joining the French Foreign Legion without the same long-term commitment or hardship. Some reporters, though, once they have covered one conflict, find the experience so compelling that they are drawn to document war after war – and rarely write about anything else.

Journalists' accounts and academic studies of reporter motivation

In *My War Gone By, I Miss It So*, Anthony Loyd tells a story of a boyhood fascination with warfare that led him first into the British Army, and later into the field as a journalist. His is an unusual account, nevertheless containing many elements which will be familiar to anyone who has reported on conflict. He is drawn to war, but realizes that he can always leave, unlike those people whose fate he has come to write about.

> For me there was always a way out. I could go to the airport, flash that UN ID card, and get on a plane to Split. I could be in London the same day if I timed it right, and that knowledge protected me from the despair that affected Sarajevo's people.
>
> (2000: 22)

I experienced similar feelings when I was based in Gaza and, on the few occasions when it was all but impossible even for non-Palestinians to leave the territory, I got just the briefest glimpse of what it must have felt like for the people among whom I lived. My freedom to leave the Gaza Strip was only threatened a few times during the two years I lived there, always at times of increased Israeli military activity. The times when it did happen, I felt uneasy. The rest of the time, I too enjoyed the comfort of what Loyd calls the knowledge that protects you from despair.

In an age when increasing numbers of journalists covering conflict are themselves being killed (see figures from the Committee to Protect Journalists and others, referred to in Chapter 2), the question of what makes journalists agree, or even want, to put themselves at risk has demanded more academic attention. All taking *Journalists under Fire* for a title, Feinstein (2006), Tumber and Webster (2006) and Tumber and

Prentoulis (2003) consider the issue. Feinstein reports on the results of his research into the trauma suffered by journalists covering conflict. That research was based on a study he carried out in the early years of this century. I was one of his subjects. I answered his survey shortly after the conversation with the Russian soldiers, above, had taken place. As part of his quest to understand the effects of trauma, he considers motivation, noting that many of those conflict reporters who try to explain why they do what they do use 'the same descriptors employed by substance abusers to depict their highs and periods of abstinence: exhilaration, brighter colors, "my drug had been taken away from me," withdrawal symptoms' (2006: 48). It is not only academic researchers who have paid greater attention to the issue in recent years. Organizations like the Dart Center for Journalism and Trauma, and Reporters without Borders, whose website includes a section on psychological injury, offer practical help and advice to those who are affected.

Most people who have reported wars do so for a combination of the reasons I listed above, albeit in different measures. Many have a moment at which they understand, as Janine di Giovanni describes in *The Place at the End of the World: Essays from the Edge* (2006), that what they are doing sets them apart.

> One wet day in Conakry, Guinea, trying to bribe my way on to a helicopter going to Sierra Leone, which was about to blow sky high, I had a terrible epiphany: I realised I was the only person trying to get to a place that everyone else was running away from.
>
> (2006: 10)

Some will be driven more by a desire to tell the world what is happening – perhaps in the hope that such knowledge might make a difference, even hasten an end to the war and the suffering which it causes. Most reporters seem to accept that making a real difference is a rare, if welcome, occurrence. As di Giovanni concludes as she reflects on her work, 'Sometimes people reacted to what I wrote and it had some good effect; sometimes not' (ibid.: 9).

Others will be motivated mainly by the thought of their report appearing in the top slot in the evening news, or on the front page of the paper. Even if a report does end up helping civilian victims of conflict, it does not mean that that was the correspondent's main purpose. Loyd, drawing conclusions from his own experience, seems to place a personal motive before all others.

Men and women who venture to someone else's war through choice do so in a variety of guises. UN General, BBC correspondent, aid worker, mercenary: in the final analysis, they all want the same thing, a hit off the action, a walk on the dark side.

(2000: 54)

Personality-led reporting: a growing televisual trend

That sense of personal motivation seems increasingly to have been mirrored in television coverage of conflict over the last two decades. During my time at the BBC, from 1995–2010, there was a growing belief that the audience was keen to see a correspondent appear as prominently as possible in the report. The idea was that their visible presence would somehow help the audience to identify with them, and thereby enhance the credibility of their story. Maybe so – but what is the story?

Today, the only news reports that do not feature a piece to camera are those compiled in a newsroom by someone who has not been at the location shown in the story. Once – partly, but not entirely, for technical reasons – it was much more common for a reporter not to do a piece to camera. Now, if the reporter is in the place where the story is happening, it is all but unthinkable. There is a very fine line between a reporter featuring him or herself prominently in order to establish their presence, and therefore their qualification to tell us what is happening there, and a reporter getting in the way of the story which they have been sent to tell. When personality-led reporting is poorly executed, the story is slanted, and even obscured. I do not wish to appear unfairly critical of one of my former colleagues at the BBC, so I will not name them. I will nevertheless single out one report which I saw on BBC World News in 2008 as a particularly bad example of the journalist getting in the way of the audience's understanding.

The reporter was covering the story of a group of refugees who had been struck down by disease. The piece took the form of a 'rant' (a report in the form of an extended piece to camera – see previous chapter), in which the journalist walked around explaining what was happening to the refugees. 'Rants', done well, can be an extremely effective way of bringing to life a location where not much is moving; an opportunity for direct storytelling. Here, there was enough human drama for the reporter to just get out of the way, and allow the audience to try to grasp what was happening. The reporter did not get out of the way. The story may nominally have been about the refugees' fate.

Looked at objectively, it was not. The story had become 'these refugees are dangerously ill, but there is a British person wandering around near their tents'. The way that the whole report was presented gave far more emphasis to the latter fact than the former. The reporter physically obscured the audience's view and, in so doing, obstructed rather than facilitated its understanding. As Susan Carruthers observes rather witheringly of some embedding in Iraq,

> The fact of being embedded itself became 'the story', narrated by television journalists in brand new fatigues, surrounded by men in uniform against an exotic desert backdrop. That they had rather little actual news to relate was hardly the point.
>
> (2011: 135)

This kind of conflict reporting, where the coverage has become a vehicle for the correspondent much as a Hollywood movie might be for a star, may not be entirely without value, but it is at best a missed opportunity. The other kind of reporter involvement, where a journalist has some kind of clear interest in the conflict which they are covering, presents a different set of challenges. 'Remember it's not your war,' BBC producer Jo Floto said to me as I prepared to leave to take up my post in Gaza. His words were a reminder to me to keep personal opinions of the conflict out of my journalism. When it is 'your war', that is not as easily done.

September 11 and journalism in the United States

The attacks on New York and Washington on September 11 2001 marked the beginning of a new phase in US foreign policy, a new assessment of relations between the west and the Arab and Muslim world and, in journalism scholarship, extensive discussion (Tumber and Prentoulis, 2003: 226; Seib, 2008: 3; Carruthers, 2011: 219) of how that in turn affected reporting itself. In *Journalism after September 11*, Zelizer and Allan seem to assume from the outset that many, if not all, the reporters who covered the events of September 11 were traumatized by them: 'At the heart of this discussion is a notion not previously addressed in scholarship on journalism, namely that of trauma,' they say (2002: 1). 'Frequently invoked as a label for a wide range of cognitive-emotional states caused by suffering and existential pain,' they continue, it is our belief that journalists and news organizations covering the events of September 11 were wounded too. There were no detached vantage points situated 'outside' the crisis from which they could objectively observe. And indeed, as we have seen in the months that have since passed, trauma does not disappear lightly.

(ibid.)

I was not in New York, or even the United States, on September 11 but, by the afternoon of 14 September, I was in Manhattan, close to 'ground zero' as the site where the twin towers of the World Trade Center had once stood came to be known. Although there were few 'detached vantage points' from which to report the story, it is not, I think, true to say that there were none. Or, if it was true to say that there were none, then the same argument could be made of any conflict. Attempts at objectivity are always affected by other factors. Either way, while the story itself was without precedent, the situation for journalists was not. It may have been for American journalists who had never worked beyond the US, but not for journalists in general. The assumption that 'journalists and news organizations … were wounded too' reads now rather like the view of someone who was themselves deprived of a vantage point 'from which they could objectively observe'. Zelizer and Allan's reference to 'the months that have since passed' is telling. A more measured judgement would only be likely to emerge after a greater time had passed. Nevertheless, I mention their work here as a study of an example of when, for some journalists, it could be considered 'your war'. The questions they raise about reporting the post-September 11 world are still of interest, but their analysis is hampered both by the time they were writing, and the fact that their terms of reference seem far too closely focused on a US point of view. Arriving in New York just after the attacks, I did struggle to find phrases adequate to conveying the significance of what had happened earlier that week. There was no doubt that the experience which the city had endured was deeply traumatic. I spent the afternoon of Sunday 16 September talking to people seeking news of their relatives at a makeshift information exchange a short distance from the smoking ruins of part of New York's skyline. Photographs of the missing were posted on noticeboards at the side of the street. The belief, confidently stated by several whom I met, that they would find their loved ones, was deeply sad.

Although my professional experience makes it difficult for me to share some of Zelizer and Allan's analysis of the extent to which trauma played a role in shaping journalistic responses to the attacks, some of the arguments advanced in their, *Journalism after September 11* are worth examining. Some parts of the book are notable for their prescience. I wrote in Chapter 2 of the increasing number of casualties among journalists in conflict areas. The idea of journalists as observers who should not be targets seems sadly to have little currency. Silvio Waisbord makes special mention of this in his chapter, 'Journalism, Risk, and Patriotism', noting that in the period following the attacks of September 11, 'members of the media had plenty of reasons to feel that they were in terrorism's bull's-eye. Islamic fundamentalists showed nothing but contempt for the principles of democratic journalism' (2002: 206). This sense of self-preservation is one of the factors possibly leading journalists to think that the United States' so-called 'war on terror' was their war too: after all, Mullah Omar, as Waisbord notes, had offered money for the murder of journalists. But he also points out ways in which 'news organizations became saturated with patriotic spirit after September 11', concluding, 'It seemed as if journalistic rules cherished during "normal" times had to be suspended for journalism to do its job' (2002: 206). He convincingly summarizes the relationship he sees between journalism and patriotism: 'In patriotism, journalism finds a cultural anchor to legitimize its social function as a full card-carrying member of the national community; in journalism, patriotism has a loyal ally, a loud defender and propagandist' (ibid.: 215). This is why a good journalist must always ask themselves if it is '(their) war'.

This last description of the relationship clearly fits my category of journalism, which chooses to reject the notion that the conflict it describes is not '(its) war'. Sreberny has also written of the effect of September 11 suggesting that, 'through the narrow definition of "we" the viewer, the news violence never happens to "us". Part of the deep shock of September 11 was that "we" had become the object of violence, not its perpetrator' (2002: 223). I think that much of the reporting I saw and heard in New York in Washington in the second half of September 2001 – let us not forget that any US citizen appearing on screen then without a stars-and-stripes lapel badge was likely to have been shouted down as callous, or even an enemy – suggested that the effect which Sreberny describes also influenced coverage. The 'we' could apply to reporters as well as members of the audience. Thus there was pressure on journalists from both belligerents in the 'war on terror': the United States seeking to mobilize support for its cause, and its enemies, such as Mullah Omar, promoting the idea that journalists should be murdered. These factors, and others – patriotic reporting was not purely the result of pressure from the US authorities, many journalists were happy to volunteer – meant that in the aftermath of September 11 there was a part of western journalism that very much saw the 'war on terror' as its war. The fact that one front of that 'war on terror', the invasion of Iraq, is seen more and more widely as having been a bad, or, at least, flawed, adventure shows that this 'my war too' journalism also had its flaws. Carruthers makes an important point about the way the initial invasion of Afghanistan, in the autumn of 2001 was covered:

> Afghanistan soon became stamped as a *victory*, at least by US media. The prematurity of this verdict should have been (and was) obvious to those observing the tenuous grip of Afghanistan's new, US-backed rulers over the country as a whole.
>
> (2011: 219) (italics in original)

I will examine the idea of the extent to which journalists in wartime balance their humanity with their role as reporters later in this chapter. On the experience of covering the aftermath of September 11, I would not think of myself then, or now, as 'wounded' by the experience. Perhaps that is because, as a European journalist who had previously covered conflict in the former Soviet Union and the Middle East, I did not necessarily share the 'trauma' from which Zelizer and Allan seem convinced that news organizations suffered – and there are plenty of other journalists, including some from the United States, who feel the same way. As Tumber and Prentoulis observe, 'Those covering September 11 were not necessarily war/foreign correspondents and, as such, may have had less experience in dealing with the anxiety, fear, and trauma associated with the coverage of catastrophic events on this scale' (2003: 226).

This sense of trauma was not new for journalists. Vassily Grossman experienced it when wondering about the fate of his mother under Nazi occupation (he later discovered that she had, as he suspected, been killed by invading German troops). In Gaza in 2009, Palestinian journalists achieved international prominence in a way that had not previously been available to them.

Case study 3: the reporting of Israel's assault on Gaza in January 2009

As noted in the preceding chapter, during 'Operation Cast Lead', Israel prevented international reporters from entering the Gaza Strip. The decision was taken on the grounds of security and, despite a ruling from Israel's Supreme Court that journalists should be allowed to enter Gaza, it remained in force. CNN and the BBC, along with other international organizations who were shut out of Gaza, expressed their frustration.

Israel's media restrictions have prevented dozens of international journalists from entering Gaza, where the Jewish state is waging an operation against militant targets.

International news media are forced to report on the more than two-week-old conflict from a hill near the Gaza–Israel border. CNN relies on a local journalist in Gaza, but cannot send other reporters into the Palestinian territory (CNN, 2009).

Three weeks after the assault began, the BBC's World News editor, Jon Williams, wrote on his blog:

> True, the BBC did manage a short trip into Gaza last week; a BBC cameraman was taken in to Northern Gaza by the IDF[21] to witness their operations. Embedding with the military is a useful piece of the jigsaw – whether in Gaza, Afghanistan or Iraq – but it is not [sic] substitute for independent, eyewitness reporting.
>
> (Williams, 2009)

The eyewitness reporting fell to those Palestinians – a now unnamed 'local journalist', in CNN's case – who more usually worked with the correspondents whom major international news organizations deployed to the territory from time to time. From their usual roles as translators, fixers and field producers, they were pushed into the spotlight as on-screen, and on-air, news reporters. The BBC journalists who came to feature so extensively in the corporation's coverage of the offensive were Rushdi Abou Alouf and Hamada Abu Qammar.[22] I worked with them both when I was based in Gaza as the BBC's correspondent. Throughout this book, I have tried as far as possible to discuss issues of journalism theory and scholarship in the light of my own experience. I have never filed a report while the street where I lived with my family was under attack. Because I have no experience to compare with that of those Palestinian journalists who covered the assault on Gaza, I switch my focus now to them.

With a population of around 1.5 million (BBC News, 2011) living in an area measuring approximately 45 kilometres by 10, Gaza is one of the most densely populated territories in the world. Government and military buildings – potential targets for the Israelis – lie next to civilian homes. There are few places in which civilians can feel safe. Both Abou

Alouf and Abu Qammar were able to bring a personal element to their reporting – for no other reason than that they themselves sensed imminent danger, as these extracts from the BBC website at the time of the offensive show:

> I was at home in Gaza City, about 200m from the Hamas education ministry, which was hit last night.
> We stayed away from the windows. We leave them open because the glass breaks if the Israelis bomb nearby, so it is very cold. It was hard to keep my four-year-old son calm.
>
> (Abou Alouf, 2009a)

> People are even leaving areas without links to Hamas, because they are expecting air strikes to hit civilian places.
> Last night two houses in Nuseirat were completely destroyed, but nobody was in either of them at the time. One belonged to a Hamas militant. The other house belonged to a political leader from the PFLP [Popular Front for the Liberation of Palestine].
> My house is next to a Hamas leader's house, so if it is hit, my house will be rubble too. That's why we're at my brother's.
>
> (Abu Qammar, 2009)

We expatriate correspondents cannot imagine what this must feel like. Many of us have been in extremely dangerous situations, close to buildings or people that were the targets of military operations. We have not done this with our families nearby, in the same danger as we ourselves were. This kind of reporting has not really been seen in western Europe since the Second World War. No one of a later generation of correspondents has really experienced that sense of very high stakes; of being so acutely involved in the action which you are describing; of being torn, presumably, between one's duty as a reporter, a citizen and a parent. That is why that particular phase of the conflict between Israel and the Palestinians marked such an important moment. It brought to a wider audience voices that they were not used to hearing, in more than one sense of the word. In the English-language media, Palestinian accents were common enough when they spoke the words of contributors to others' reports; they were less familiar when they were the words of the reporter him or herself. The convention, especially in covering the Israeli–Palestinian conflict for western international media (although not the case for Arab media), of letting an outsider cover the story, was broken by the enforced absence of international correspondents.

Audiences learnt immediately that something new or unusual was happening. Those new accents brought new perspectives. With the newsgathering resources restricted by the Israeli ban on journalists entering Gaza, and further restrictions imposed upon movement within the territory, those journalists who were able to work had to find imaginative ways of doing so.

Abou Alouf and Abu Qammar were among those who can now almost be considered pioneers of this new kind of conflict reporting, forged partly from forces which prevented things from being any other way, and, partly from the fact that, once those forces did begin to dictate the working environment, major news organizations remembered that they did actually have untapped talent among their Palestinian staff. Their knowledge and experience, instead of being used to inform the coverage of non-Palestinian colleagues from outside the territory, was used as raw material for their own reportage. Their familiarity with the streets where they had grown up, and which they had followed so frequently (Gazans' lack of freedom of movement means that very few ever travel beyond the territory; some hardly within it), allowed them to seek out the places that would enable them to tell the story in a way an outsider could not. Abou Alouf's report *Inside Gaza* from 16 January 2009 was a fine example of this. His series of short reports featured a series of locations affected by the fighting: Gaza City's main hospital; a shopping street briefly busy during the daily truce which was called to allow civilians to buy provisions; a school outbuilding in which three members of one family had been killed during an Israeli attack; and a playground where, in the weak winter sunshine, the primary schoolchildren of this conflict-ravaged coastal strip cautiously used the occasional pre-announced lull in the fighting to go on the swings and the slides.

What did this bring audiences that they had not previously had? In one sense, the same material – civilian hardship in time of war – which any responsible journalist would include in his or her report was provided, even if it was delivered in a different way. In another sense, the fact that the majority of the BBC and others correspondents were kept out of the territory meant that the live broadcasts, which are often such a drain on a reporter's time as far as pure newsgathering is concerned, were taken care of by those who were forced to remain at a distance from the action. That allowed Abou Alouf and his fellow Palestinian journalists to report from places where, in normal circumstances, they might simply have been deployed to phone in facts and figures. The As-Shifa Hospital is one such place.

When I was the BBC's correspondent in Gaza, my need to broadcast as many as four times an hour during a breaking news story meant that there were occasions when I did not leave my office to see what was happening for myself. Sometimes, that did not matter. I justified this by the fact that, as the only resident non-Palestinian reporter working in the territory, my accumulated knowledge of areas and ongoing situations, combined with the excellent network of sources which the bureau had cultivated, meant that I did not need to go to the site of every single Israeli attack in order to assess its consequences. Both my apartment, where I had a facility to broadcast in quality, and the BBC office, were close to the centre of Gaza City, so there were times when the conflict unfolded literally around the corner. Once, after I had completed my posting to the territory, the tower block in which the BBC's office was situated was even struck by an Israeli missile (aimed apparently at a Hamas-affiliated media organization which had offices on a lower floor). Because of the extensive broadcasting requests which a breaking story frequently involved for me, more usually one of the producers from the BBC bureau would go to the hospital to relay to me, and my colleague Fayed Abushammala from the BBC Arabic service, the latest casualty figures.

This kind of reporting would have been better done from the hospital by the correspondent him or herself, but the logistical constraints of sending constant updates in broadcast quality made this all but impossible. When Abou Alouf, freed from the constraints of continuous live reports, was able to head out to tell the story of his Gaza, he started his story in the casualty department of the As-Shifa Hospital. This is the 'rant' at its most memorable and effective: the reporter is present to explain and interpret, but not to obscure. Although he is in shot most of the time, we the audience see enough of the action of the hospital emergency department to understand that countless casualties are being brought in and that, behind the curtains which surround the beds, people are dying of wounds which defied the doctors' exhausted hands and minds. Abou Alouf's authoritative narration, mostly on camera, sometimes off, is an example of how this technique is best used, rather than the woeful case to which I referred earlier in this chapter.

This was a very testing time for those Palestinian journalists who found themselves thrust into the glare of international news. 'I will never forget these days. It was like a horrible twenty-two days: personally, and in terms of work, also,' Abu Qammar recalls (Telephone interview, 21 December 2010). 'The hardest thing was when you have to think of work, and also to think of the family.'

Abu Qammar is from the Nuseirat refugee camp in the centre of the Gaza Strip. As the Israeli assault intensified, he found himself cut off from Gaza City, and therefore from the main focus of the story. Eventually, he decided that he had to leave his family, and try to get to Gaza City. As mentioned in the extract above from one of his reports from that time, his family had already left their home, which they feared might be hit because of its proximity to the house of a Hamas member.

> That was really hard for me in personal level, to leave my family and my kids, evacuated in other people's houses, and to decide to go to the work, because I believed at that time, I believed that was the moment. Because if I didn't cover the story properly and professionally from Gaza, then I shouldn't be in my position, and I shouldn't be working as a journalist, even, or in journalism. That was really a very hard decision to take.

Once he had succeeded in getting to Gaza City, he found a place where food was in short supply. The bakeries had no bread. Fruit and vegetables, most of which are produced in the south of the territory – now cut off by the Israeli Army – were scarce, and expensive. Abu Qammar, who had previously been with his family, but cut off from the main scene of the story, now found himself cut off from his family.

> I mean I didn't have time to think even of my family during the war, because I had to think of a way or another to cover the story properly. So that was really a terrible time for my family actually, who are stuck in the other half of the Gaza Strip.
>
> (ibid.)

He says that his intention was to be a journalist above all – even if that meant balancing that with the challenges of being a person, and a parent.

> I am a Palestinian, but during the war I avoided being a Palestinian, and I was just looking for telling the facts, the truth of what's happening on the ground. And that was really difficult, because at the same time I have to think of my family, who were evacuated from my house, to other, neighbouring, families.
>
> (ibid.)

Abu Qammar reflects that getting the airtime, which, had they not been banned from the territory, would have fallen to non-Palestinian staff, also brought exacting demands. He says he strove to observe the editorial ethics of the international news organization which employed him and Abou Alouf. 'At that time there was no foreign correspondents in Gaza, and we, as the BBC employees, we tried to be really impartial' (ibid.). That was especially hard when they were required to appear on air at the same time as spokespeople for the Israeli government or military – representatives of the people who were putting their families in such great danger. 'This was difficult for a local journalist to do,' Abu Qammar admits, but adds,

> working for the BBC for almost ten years now, we got an experience, we know how others look at the story. We have a little bit of experience in covering these situations, but the war was really awful at the end.
>
> (ibid.)

For all the hardship and difficulty involved, Abu Qammar is satisfied that he fulfilled his role as a reporter as he had hoped to when he took the decision to head to Gaza City and leave his family in the refugee camp. 'At the end I was really, you know, very proud because I succeeded to cover, with my colleague of course, I succeeded to cover the story properly for tv, for radio, for online' (ibid.).

But, as Feinstein's research demonstrated, the experience of covering war is draining not only for the professional journalist, but also for the person that journalist is. 'I never cried. As a person, I never cried. I don't know. I felt I had a problem at that time,' Abu Qammar concludes, looking back two years later. 'Maybe because from the beginning I decided to avoid myself from being a Palestinian, and to be a journalist, at that time, it was really difficult' (ibid.).

Personal reflections on practice: the journalist as professional, and person

Some might argue with my suggestion that western reporters have not experienced anything like this since the Second World War. Were not the attacks of September 11 in New York and Washington, the attacks in Madrid, London, Mumbai and elsewhere just as traumatic for the reporters involved? Even if some journalists choose not to identify with the soldiers – their compatriots or their allies – whom they accompany in Iraq or Afghanistan – does not the patriotic defence correspondent have the right to do so, to talk about 'our troops'? Perhaps so, in the case of the latter example, and not for a moment would I question the suggestion that some reporters were traumatized by covering the attacks on western cities. I was in London on 7 July 2005, when suicide bombers attacked the transport system during morning rush hour. I found the sensation of my adopted home city being under attack profoundly unsettling but, if I am honest, I think that I and many other residents of London were probably resigned to the fact that there would be suicide bombings in the city sooner or later. That lessened, although did not prevent, the shock when it came.

That is different from the feeling that your town is under attack by a force whose offensive weapons hugely outgun the defences your city or territory can call upon: the sensation of the people of Grozny, Gaza or, latterly, Misrata. Working alongside such people – people whose war it indisputably is – brings particular challenges for the expatriate journalist covering conflict. For the people who surround the reporter, the danger is not a planned attack which may or may not be stopped before it happens. Danger is an army that is able to attack their city almost unchallenged because their guns and numbers are so much greater than those of their targets. When you are reporting from such a place, these are the people who are your guide, your translator; theirs are the eyes and ears that enable your own to understand and interpret what they see and hear. In Gaza or Grozny, you have to share their impressions and hear their views, and yet somehow strive to put them in context, all the while remembering that your presence there is temporary; your stake in what unfolds before you vastly lower than theirs, apart from at moments of extreme danger, when death for you all would render such differences irrelevant.

This is another time, like those I mentioned in Chapter 2, when the reporter in a war zone has a perspective shared by no one else. You are a source of news to those around you as well as those from whom you are separated by vast distances. It can be awkward. In Gaza, having learned, through our established, reliable sources in the Palestinian security apparatus, of an Israeli attack, my first move would be to telephone the Israeli Army spokesperson's office for a comment. Sometimes, if the success or otherwise of their operation was not yet known, the spokesperson would refuse to comment, or confirm 'off the record' only that they were aware that it was in progress. Then they might ask me what I had learned of it – the as yet unreported words of

Palestinian security sources were of interest to them, after all – and any English speaker within earshot of me as I made the call from Gaza would ask me the same question too once I had come off the phone with the Israeli military. My rule when answering these questions from whichever side was to stick to saying only what I would say on air, with the exception that in private conversation with someone standing next to me I might add whether or not I believed what I had been told. These were occasions when you sometimes had to take a step back; where the internal struggle between personal and professional was sometimes difficult to manage. You wanted to be able to agree with the people who had given you so much help that without them you would not have had a story that day; and yet you knew that your report would almost certainly, in the interests of balance, have to contain the accounts of their enemies, the accounts of people whom they distrusted or hated, accounts which they held to be untrue.

There are reporters who arrive in a conflict as outsiders but who come to take sides, or at least to be seen to do so. Sometimes, this bias is imagined by their detractors, like the experience I wrote of in Chapter 1 of the journalist from the United States working in Tbilisi, whose interlocutors suspected him of failing to tell the truth simply because he was willing to report points of view other than theirs. Others are moved by a sense of injustice to identify with the plight or the cause of those whose story they initially came to tell, rather than play a role in. I cannot think of any examples where a reporter has actually taken up arms in a conflict which they had come to cover as an outsider, even though there are plenty of documented cases of journalists using weapons, and, no doubt, even more undocumented ones. In Vietnam, during the Tet offensive, Michael Herr, in his own words 'slid over to the wrong end of the story', firing a gun to provide cover for a group of soldiers seeking to return to his position. Referring to the danger involved in this situation, he concludes, 'we were in the Alamo, no place else, and I wasn't a reporter, I was a shooter' (1977: 60). Morrison and Tumber (1988: 96) describe British journalists deciding to carry guns in case they find themselves in a similar position. Despite being written more than twenty years ago about a conflict thirty years ago, Morrison and Tumber's chapter '"It's All Right; I Am British, After All" – A Theory of Change and a Change in Theory' in *Journalists at War* (1988) still has a striking relevance today for the clarity with which they define the pressure which reporters can feel to identify with the troops they accompany. 'It was not just a question of sharing the moods of the troops through shared experience, but of actively beginning to identify with them by being part of the whole exercise' (ibid.: 97).

If there are no known cases of reporters taking up arms in the cause of those they came to write about, rather than fight for, there are other cases of intervention. Perhaps one of the most famous of recent years has been that of Michael Nicholson, the veteran reporter for Independent Television News in the UK, who adopted a nine-year-old orphan, Natasha, whom he met in Bosnia. Nicholson later told the story in a book which in turn inspired the film, *Welcome to Sarajevo* (1997). Few correspondents have gone to this length, but the question of the extent to which one should intervene, even to offer basic assistance, is an eternal one, with no obvious answers. It is, though, one which seems of great interest to audiences who have not themselves been to conflict zones.

Conclusion: report the story, don't become it

On occasions when, as a working journalist, I went to speak to groups of journalism students, I was almost always asked how you decide the extent to which you will get involved, even if that just means helping people. My opinion is that you are where you are to tell people what is happening. You are an observer. That does not mean that you cannot offer water, food or first aid to people (the chances are that you may well be better supplied than those around you). What I feel is less justifiable is then to go on to film – as some correspondents have done – the charitable act, and include it in your report. This is one of those cases, like the refugee camp, above, where a journalist tries to become the story, rather than report it. The result is that the story delivered to the audience runs roughly as follows: the war has deprived many people of food, water and adequate medical care, but it is not as bad as all that because a man from a TV channel in a wealthy country is on the spot to give the refugees some supplies from his car. The audience learns little more than that the reporter wants to be seen as caring. I now spend much of my working week trying to explain to journalism students that a news story must concentrate on that which is most important to the audience. That kind of report fails the test.

At the other end of the scale, and to answer the students' frequent question more fully, a good journalist must never forget that he or she is a human being too. Preparing to begin my assignment in Gaza, I drew on my most distressing experience as a journalist: covering the wars in

Chechnya. I steeled myself to expect that sort of horror on a daily basis, and only later realised that the conflict in Gaza was something quite different: longer-lasting certainly, offering less chance of escape to somewhere else, but also less intense. The number of dead alone speaks for itself. If thousands have died in the last two or three decades of the Israeli–Palestinian conflict – the majority of them Palestinian – then tens of thousands died in Chechnya in a much shorter period.

I wonder now with hindsight if I prepared myself too rigorously and if, as a result, some of my reporting lacked compassion. If that is the case, then I did so for one simple reason: self-protection. Professor Feinstein's questions, in the document he circulated to collect material for his study, were never far from my mind. I was worried about the effect that living and working in Gaza would have on me, not only as a reporter, but as a person. Sometimes it is hard to remember that you are writing for people, the majority of whom have never been in a war zone. There is part of you that says, 'This is a war, and terrible things happen in war. That is just how it is.' As a result, you can appear to play down death, and the destruction of homes and workplaces, as some-thing commonplace. There is a danger, in such situations, that a reporter will just fall into what Susan Carruthers has warned against: 'explaining violence as inexplicable' (2000: 44–5). Engagement can also be problematic. Waisbord's verdict on American journalism after September 11, 'It seemed as if journalistic rules cherished during "normal" times had to be suspended for journalism to do its job' (2002: 206), should serve as a warning. In such cases, as in some of the jingo-istic reporting of the capture of Saddam Hussein, journalism fails to do its job. When, as in the case of the BBC's Palestinian journalists in Gaza, reporters resist that urge to suspend journalistic rules despite their personal interest in the conflict, journalism succeeds.

Retaining sound judgement while in great danger is at times beyond almost all reporters. In that sense, reporting conflict has something in common with other roles which people fulfil in time of war: their tasks may be difficult at the best of times (really good reporting is never easy) but they must be carried out to the highest standard in places where simply surviving can be hard enough. In recent years, new factors have arisen to complicate a reporter's involvement in conflict even further. New technology – and new ways of working – have not compensated. It has to be admitted – as I heard senior news executives concede at that event some months after the Israeli decision to ban journalists from Gaza during their offensive – that the tactic, like the one adopted by the Sri Lankan military during an assault on the Tamil Tigers some months later, had been successful from the authorities' point of view. The same may come to be said of Syria's decision to ban foreign journalists during the unrest in 2011. What is the answer for journalism in those sorts of situations? Remembering Michael Herr's reflections (1977: 175), quoted in the last chapter, on the limits of conventional journalism, I would like now to look at ways in which conflict journalism could evolve in order to reveal war in a more effective way.

Summary

- journalists' motives for covering war include a desire for adventure, duty, patriotism and the hope of career advancement
- personality-led reporting
- September 11 and journalism in the US
- case study: Palestinian journalists report Israel's assault on Gaza in January 2009 for international media
- journalists who come to identify with troops
- conflict reporter: journalist, human being or both?

7 Not as simple as 'death or glory': the future

You only report death or glory and nothing in between. And it's just not like that.

(British Army Major Richard Streatfeild, interview in London, 6 January 2011)

Journalists are often accused of oversimplification. They cannot win this war of words with their critics. Specialists shout them down for missing significant detail. If journalists include too much of that detail, they are criticized for producing work that has become inaccessible to the general reader. These questions defy simple solutions. The best editorial decisions devolve from sound judgement – influenced by professional ideas of objectivity and impartiality (as discussed in Chapter 3), and by guidelines on taste and decency (also discussed in Chapter 3) – not by following a book of rules. Yet those decisions can only be taken on the basis of the material that the reporter or the editor has in front of him or her as the deadline approaches. If that material is flawed or incomplete, so too will be the story delivered to the audience.

The run-up to the 2003 invasion of Iraq: reflections on an incomplete story

The US-led invasion of Iraq is the most important recent example of an incomplete story. I should declare that I opposed the invasion. I feared it would lead to greater instability in the region and, while I agreed with the view that the world would be a better place without Saddam Hussein as leader of Iraq, I feared that achieving that goal by invading the country would cause too many civilian deaths. At the time, I wondered if my opinion was influenced by the fact that I was living in Gaza. I had arrived there in August 2002, a little more than six months before the invasion. Many people in Gaza admired Saddam Hussein for his implacable opposition to Israel. The time, during the war of 1991, when Iraq had fired missiles at Israel was remembered by some Gazans as a time of celebration. I wondered if being exposed to such views had led me to doubt the suggestion, advanced most prominently by neo-conservatives in the administration of President George W. Bush, that troops invading the country would be welcomed as liberators. It is almost difficult now to recall the climate of opinion at the time when, as Susan Carruthers says, 'US journalists did much to bolster the administration's claim that Saddam Hussein still harboured a significant cache of weapons of mass destruction' (2011: 29) and 'news channels also contributed to the growing popular conviction that Iraq was connected to Al-Qaeda' (ibid.: 30). Nor was this a problem for US media alone (Miller, 2004: 3). As a BBC journalist, I respected the corporation's requirement that its journalists be impartial (see BBC Editorial Guidelines, 2010c for the current version). I never expressed my opposition to the coming war in anything but private conversation or correspondence.

At the time, the only occasion I found myself in Iraq was in 1992 when, as a producer for Reuters TV, I entered the country illegally across the northern border. The Kurdish people of northern Iraq were holding elections. They had in effect been granted autonomy following the war of 1990–1. Saddam Hussein's government had no real power in the region. The Kurds, despite their *de facto* separation from the rest of the country, still remained deeply fearful of Saddam. They described the fate of those who had opposed his regime. They took me to see empty and burnt-out police stations which they said had been places of torture and execution. As a British journalist, whose country had just been part of the coalition that had driven Saddam Hussein from Kuwait, I hardly dared think what might happen to me had I fallen into unfriendly hands. So my opposition to the war had not evolved because I was some kind of useful idiot who failed to see the merciless tyranny presided over by Saddam Hussein. Aside from my obligation to be impartial, one reason why I did not make my opposition public was that I was not sure that I was right. My conviction was deeply held but, given my lack of experience and firsthand knowledge of Iraq, not based on sound evidence so much as on opinion formed while living in Gaza. Still, I strongly felt that we were not getting the full story – and subsequent analysis of the way the build-up to the war was reported, such as the *New York Times*' admission, which I discuss below, that it had fallen for 'misinformation', suggest that I was right. The UK media were hardly innocent. In their study of supportive coverage in the British media during the Iraq war, Robinson *et al.* conclude, 'Press and television news relied heavily on coalition sources and supportive battle coverage prevailed even among newspapers that had opted to oppose the war' (2010: 104). Of their study of media coverage in the pre-invasion phase, Tumber and Palmer argue that more attention should have been given to two significant matters: 'the alleged links between the Saddam regime and Osama bin Laden' (2004: 91) and 'the question of the US motives for going to war' (ibid.: 92). Many people have probably forgotten the first of those, so entirely has the idea been discredited in the intervening years. The second, including the idea of weapons of mass destruction, is never far from any discussion of the rights and wrongs of the war – for the simple reason that the invaders never found such weapons.

So how could coverage have been made more comprehensive? Could journalists, for example, have tried to gather the views of ordinary Iraqis? They could have tried, but the extent to which it would have been a worthwhile exercise is questionable. The oppressed citizens of a murderous police state are unlikely to speak frankly to foreign journalists when those same foreign journalists are accompanied by agents of that same murderous police state. And who are ordinary Iraqis? Arab or Kurd? Shia or Sunni? Farmer or pharmacist? Still, something more could have been done to try to give us, not just us journalists, but us citizens and voters, a fuller picture. For that is what we needed, and what we need and will need in the kind of conflicts that we are called on to cover in the post-Cold War, post-September 11 world. In *Supermedia*, Charlie Beckett explains, 'What we are striving for here is what I call "Editorial Diversity". Essentially, this is an openness to engage with new sources, perspectives, and narratives, and an ability to use them to create networked journalism' (2008: 150). The best journalism always succeeds in telling its audience something that they did not previously know. That can be new information, or a fresh and illuminating analysis of what is already established. The best journalism, in other words, should enlighten, or even challenge, its audience. News should not just be, as Evelyn Waugh's character Corker defines it in *Scoop*, 'what a chap who doesn't care much about anything wants to read about' (1938: 66). News is not just an attempt to give people what they want, but also, especially in the case of public-service media, to give them what they need. Now it seems that technology offers us unprecedented opportunity to draw on a wider range of sources to inform good journalism, to improve the way in which we report conflict. In peacetime, the cost to democracy of failing to do so is great. In wartime, it is a matter of life and death. Decisions taken for the wrong reasons, or as a result of wishful thinking, can lead to actions that cause people to be killed. In Chapter 4, I referred to doubts over the extent to which reporting can really influence government policy, the 'CNN effect'. All the same, news media, and therefore a public, which are either not in possession of the full facts, or at least not using them, be that deliberately or through incompetence, cannot influence things for the better. Those who are in possession of complete information may still not be able to influence events for the better – but they have a much stronger chance than those who do not.

This was especially true of the incomplete reporting of the Iraq war. The *New York Times'* admission that it was 'taken in' (2004) over the real prospects for the US military campaign in Iraq is still striking in its frankness years after it was published. Nowhere in the British media was there as high-profile an acceptance of error committed as there was in the *New York Times* – even though, as Tumber and Palmer have pointed out in the extract quoted above, the British media cannot all claim to have questioned the motives for war to a sufficient extent. In May 2004, the newspaper carried an article entitled '*The Times* and Iraq', under the byline 'From the Editors'. The subject was a review of the coverage of the Iraq war. 'In some cases,' the piece stated, 'information that was controversial then, and seems questionable now, was insufficiently qualified or allowed to stand unchallenged.' The article went on:

> The problematic articles varied in authorship and subject matter, but many shared a common feature. They depended at least in part on information from a circle of Iraqi informants, defectors and exiles bent on 'regime change' in Iraq, people whose credibility has come under increasing public debate in recent weeks. (The most prominent of the anti-Saddam campaigners, Ahmad Chalabi, has been named as an occasional source in *Times* articles since at least 1991, and has introduced reporters to other exiles. He became a favourite of hard-liners within the Bush administration and a paid broker of information from Iraqi exiles, until his payments were cut off last week.) Complicating matters for journalists, the accounts of these exiles were often eagerly confirmed by United States officials convinced of the need to intervene in Iraq. Administration officials now acknowledge that they sometimes fell for misinformation from these exile sources. So did many news organizations — in particular, this one.

In one sense, the *New York Times* was 'taken in' as a result of its own failure to follow the most basic rules of journalism. They failed to seek opposing views to the ones with which they were presented by official sources. They sought 'confirmation' of these already flawed views from one source which could be all but guaranteed to 'eagerly' confirm them: those ideologically driven, neo-conservative members of the US administration who were apparently convinced that their proposed invasion of Iraq would bring tremendous political and economic benefit. Journalism is not just about seeking opposing views though. It is about seeking the widest possible range of views and selecting the most relevant from among them. Even if it were unrealistic to conduct an extended vox pop among the people of Iraq, there were other Iraqi sources – and people apart from US officials from whom to seek confirmation of stories. As Nick Davies wrote of suspect stories from Fallujah in the aftermath of the invasion, 'each of them needed to be checked; and if there was no evidence, then each of them should have been chucked' (2008: 253–4). More recently, Franklin and Carlson have drawn attention to 'the question of access to the news and the mixture of voices that regularly appear – as well as who is left out' (2011: 2). Those news organizations that 'fell for misinformation' failed to consider this question of 'who is left out' sufficiently, if at all.

In the aftermath of the invasion, Salam Pax, 'The Baghdad blogger', became feted in the established news media – at least in some of those which eschewed blatant jingoism – writing for the *Guardian*, and making filmed reports for the BBC. His entries written in the months before the invasion still give us a valuable insight into what it felt like for residents of Baghdad as they realized that their city was to be attacked by the US military and its allies. Details about the hazards of bomb shelters, and the increasing fortification of the city (Pax, 2003) seem to me exactly what Charlie Beckett has in mind when he writes about 'new sources, perspectives, and narratives'. Should not the major news organizations have sought out more of these, in addition to their 'circle of Iraqi informants, defectors and exiles bent on "regime change" in Iraq'? For media who were unquestioningly supportive of the war, the answer is probably 'no' – only because it would not have suited their editorial agenda. For other media, with a more rigorous approach to providing a wider perspective, the answer must be yes. So why was this not done to a greater extent? Of course, there were the practical difficulties of gaining access to people in Iraq, noted above, and the eternal pressures of time and resources. These are not sufficient excuses. As the BBC noted in its document *From Seesaw to Wagon Wheel: Safeguarding*

Impartiality in the 21st Century, 'In today's multi-polar Britain, with its range of cultures, beliefs and identities, impartiality involves many more than two sides to an argument' (BBC Trust, 2007: 5). The same was true of the run-up to the invasion of Iraq. More voices should have been heard. The gravest possible consequence would have been the use of sources that were unreliable, or deliberately set out to mislead. And that is what happened in any case.

To try to redress some of these shortcomings, conflict journalism needs to do two things: strictly observe long-standing best practice, and adapt it to current circumstances. In other words, especially in these times when new technology offers a bewildering array of sources, reporters need to check them. For what is the *New York Times'* piece 'From the Editors' if not a recognition that they had failed to follow the approach drilled into every trainee or first-year journalism student? In undertaking that task, journalists can make the very best of the opportunities offered by improved global communications.

Soldiers' stories seeing the light of day: Major Richard Streatfeild and the BBC

I began this book with the story of my ancestor, James Russell, at the Battle of Waterloo. His account of his experience, I pointed out, predated that of his pioneering, professional war-correspondent namesake, William Howard Russell. My ancestor's letter was written to reassure his family that he had survived 'a most Bloody Battle with the French as ever was fought'. I do not know exactly how the letter reached my ancestor's family, although I assume it was not subject to any form of military censorship. I also assume that, at the time of writing, it was not intended for publication. It does, however, tell us much about the circumstances of an ordinary cavalryman and his experience in one of the most important battles in European history. His account, as I say, was not intended for publication but, if we are to report conflict more completely in our age, its contemporary equivalents could be.

From the autumn of 2009 until the spring of 2010, the BBC's *Today* programme broadcast an unusual series of reports from Afghanistan. They were written and presented by Richard Streatfeild, a Major in the British Army.

> I always had a view that maybe as soldiers we weren't as good at explaining to people, to a broader audience, what it was that we were

going through on a day to day basis. There were very few genuine voices from the front line coming through,

Streatfeild told me in an interview in London on 6 January 2011, some months after his return. All subsequent quotations are taken from this interview. He told me that his audio diary had come about as the result of a conversation with a friend of his brother who was a BBC producer, recalling that he had told the BBC journalist, 'You only report death or glory and nothing in between. And it's just not like that.' Streatfeild said that his purpose was to explain what life was like for soldiers in order to increase public understanding.

I wanted to give a flavour of the absolute reality of how soldiers behave on operations, because, going back to my original start point, how can the public be expected to know how soldiers behave on operations if someone doesn't explain to them what's happening?

Naturally, this was not a straightforward relationship. It seems there was a lengthy delay between the idea first being discussed, and its becoming reality. Streatfeild recalls initial apprehension, from both the BBC and the ministry of defence (MOD) as to how the relationship would work.

When we had our first meeting we were all quite nervous about each other. I was quite nervous that I wouldn't be able to provide what they were looking for, and that I wouldn't necessarily have the time to do it. The BBC were quite nervous about getting pure unadulterated propaganda from a military source – unchecked, and not being able to be there to corroborate what I was saying. And the MOD were naturally a little nervous about unleashing an untried, untested military officer onto a media channel that was very high profile.

In *The First Casualty*, his definitive history of the war correspondent, Phillip Knightley notes, of the time prior to William Howard Russell's deployment,

Before the Crimea, British editors either stole war news from foreign newspapers, or employed junior officers to send letters from the battlefront, a most unsatisfactory arrangement. For not only were these soldier-correspondents highly selective in what they wrote, regarding themselves first as soldiers and then as correspondents;

they also understood little of the workings of newspapers, or even of what constituted 'news'.

(1989: 4)

Streatfeild rejects the idea of himself as an 'officer journalist', or 'soldier-correspondent', as Knightley puts it. He says that he wanted to speak to relatives more than the general reader.

I certainly didn't feel like an 'officer journalist,' I just felt that, we always do, most officers – I'd say ninety-nine per cent – write some kind of weekly, monthly, letter to families back at home, saying pretty much what I was saying on Radio 4. And the fact that those never see the light of day in journalistic terms – I was just extremely lucky to have a friend of my brother's who was a producer on Radio 4, the happy alignment of the planets that meant that I could explain to more people. But I definitely felt that the audience, my principal audience for the blog, was always the families of the soldiers that I was commanding.

In that respect, he shared the purpose of my ancestor: to inform, perhaps more importantly to reassure, those who mattered most to the serviceman or woman in a dangerous place far from home. In one sense, his contribution to our understanding of the conflict is the modern equivalent of James Russell's letter home. In others, it is something significantly different. As Streatfeild himself explains, his broadcasts were only able to go ahead after meetings between the BBC and the MOD. Streatfeild had himself formerly worked in the army's public relations department, so he was aware of the editorial priorities and requirements of anything published under the name of a serving officer. In other words, even if his time was short when he was writing and recording them, and he did not have the time to draft and rewrite, his broadcasts were carefully prepared. In that sense, they are clearly distinct from both my ancestor's letter, and the 'weekly, monthly, letter' which Streatfeild speaks of other soldiers sending. His contributions may have been inspired by these earlier models, but they were meant, from their very conception, as texts that were supposed to be made public, and that were aimed at particular audiences. Clearly, the families of the service personnel seem to have been uppermost in Streatfeild's mind as he wrote and recorded but, while they may have been the primary target audience, they were not the only one. For Streatfeild is clear that he was talking to the wider public too, trying to 'explain to them what's happening'. He understood that his ability to do so on the BBC was something the BBC would have concerns about – this was something new and out of the ordinary. As he points out, the BBC 'were quite nervous about getting pure unadulterated propaganda from a military source'. Unless a news organization completely supports, or is forced to support, the military campaign which it is covering, then a conflict of interest is constantly in play to a greater or lesser extent. Even when it does not, there could be suspicions, as there might be here, that the media organization was trying to curry favour with the government. The BBC's battles with the Labour government of Tony Blair, over the reporting of the intelligence presented to justify UK involvement in the invasion of Iraq (Robinson *et al.*, 2010: 74) were still fresh in the memory. Whether or not that was a factor here, relations between armies and reporters, as I noted in Chapter 2, often take on the feel of an uneasy game. There are clearly areas of mutual interest but, in the end, the agendas and purpose of the two differ to such an extent that they can never converge.

There are other potential problems with such an arrangement too: practical ones. Knightley writes that some of the officers whom newspapers used as contributors, in the era before William Howard Russell and other professional correspondents, could not be relied upon to send despatches. As he says, they regarded 'themselves first as soldiers and then as correspondents'. Streatfeild, as a serving officer in the modern age, naturally shared this priority. As he says, 'there was a period from January, through to about the end of February, middle of February, where we were involved in such a lot of stuff operationally that I didn't write a thing'.

That is understandable. But it also highlights the potential problems – not just the editorial ones about 'unadulterated propaganda from a military source' – attached to the use of such reports. It is hard to imagine any news organization today that would rely on a serving officer alone for content, but I include the example of Streatfeild's contributions to the BBC because it helps us to understand a way in which we can fill some of the gaps which, at present, restrict our audiences' understanding. Politics – a desire on the part of the MOD to get its message across – may have inspired its decision to go along with the plan, but technology made it a reality.

Streatfeild says his only equipment was a small voice recorder, a USB cable to transfer his work to his computer and, of course, an internet connection. His reports do have a slightly rough, out-in-the-field air about them. On at least one, I thought I heard the sound of him folding away his paper after having read from it. Recent improvements in internet connections available to serving officers were what made his contributions a feasible idea. 'Five, no maybe, six or seven years ago, not possible because we simply didn't have the bandwidth,' he says, 'it would have been possible, but only by snail mail.'

That, of course, would have made it impractical. There is another side to technological change too. Making public any aspects of military life involves a risk in an age when an enemy has no need of an ambassador reading *The Times* in Belgravia to see the latest despatch. As Streatfeild puts it, 'The enemy aren't stupid. They've got access to Facebook. So there is a security element.' So this new source of material, which news organizations like the BBC are increasingly using, is also a new battlefield in the era of information warfare. Nor is this confined to Afghanistan. In recent years, social networking websites have become a new front in the Israeli–Palestinian conflict. At least since Israel's assault on Gaza at the end of 2008 and beginning of 2009, there have been reports (*Jerusalem Post*, 2010; ynet, 2010) of both the Israeli military and Palestinian groups giving instructions to their troops and supporters to exercise extreme caution when using sites which may be a means for their enemies to gather information. As I noted in Chapter 5, Evgeny Morozov has warned of the danger that computers can be turned into 'spying machines' (2011: 170). In the 'Arab Spring' of 2011, authoritarian governments also proved adept at exploiting social media against their opponents (Preston, 2011).

Talking to terrorists: trying to tell the full story

So, if combatants should be careful only to gather, rather than to disclose, sensitive information through social networking and other websites, how should journalists use what they find there? If we are going to hear from British Army officers, we should also hear from their enemies. We should hear from them for two reasons above all: in the interests of impartiality, and in order to get as full a picture as possible of what is going on.

I understand that such a suggestion is controversial, and I understand why. I also believe that there is no alternative if we are to improve our understanding of the conflicts in our world today. As a news producer and reporter at the British commercial breakfast TV programme *GMTV* (1993–2010) in the 1990s, I experienced the effects of the absurd legislation – introduced by the Conservative government of Margaret Thatcher in 1988, and still then in force – which banned the broadcasting of the voices of representatives of Sinn Fein, the political wing of the Irish Republican Army, and ten other organizations believed to support terrorism (BBC News, 2008a). This was the last tactic in a long-running campaign to silence such voices, as Roger Bolton's (1990) and Liz Curtis's (1998) accounts testify. I use the word 'absurd' carefully, for this proscription did nothing to aid understanding. It therefore complicated, rather than assisted, public debate on the prospects for, and possible way towards, a resolution of the conflict in Northern Ireland. At its worst, it would have been simply comic – and satirists did have fun with it – had the issue it addressed not been so serious.

This incompleteness in coverage was not, of course, confined to Iraq or Northern Ireland. Stephen Somerville, who reported on the Vietnam War for Reuters, concedes,

> The problem about the Vietnamese war, the American war in Vietnam that is, in a general sense, is that it was all reported on a pretty well one-sided basis. We were reporting the South Vietnamese situation from the point of view of the Americans and the South Vietnamese largely. We, Reuters, and most other western agencies, with one or two exceptions were not reporting North Vietnam, or from North Vietnam at all. The main exception was AFP, Agence France Presse, which had a bureau in Hanoi and was allowed to report, but within a pretty limited range I should say, but they did at least do eye witness reporting on what was happening in North Vietnam, as well as putting out what the North Vietnamese wanted them to put out. The eye witness reporting by AFP was extremely valuable. Reuters never, throughout the American war, was able to get permission to have a bureau or a correspondent inside North Vietnam. So I always felt we were doing only half our job really.
>
> (Interview, London, 17 May 2011)

The political situation of the time – specifically, the North Vietnamese government's refusal to grant access to almost all western agencies – prevented Reuters from doing more than 'half (their) job'; the technology of the time meant that they were quite unable to circumvent that. Could camera phones and social networking sites have made a difference? They could but, as the Syrian authorities' ban on foreign journalists in the spring and summer of 2011 demonstrated, the effect of such technology can be limited if a government is determined to limit it.

In June 2011, Robert Gates, who was coming to the end of his time as American Defense Secretary, confirmed reports that, after waging war on them for ten years, the United States was talking to the Taliban. Gates noted, 'a political outcome is the way most of these wars end' (Stewart, 2011). In this case, as in 'most', as Gates observed, a military power accepted the need to talk to those it considered terrorists in order to seek an end to a conflict. In the same way, reporters need to seek out the views of insurgents if they are to cover an insurgency. A professional code which values impartiality should not permit a political correspondent to do a story without talking to different parties. Why should conflict journalism be different?

I do not underestimate the editorial, political and practical challenges which such an approach will necessarily involve. The editorial difficulties are all of those outlined in Chapters 3 and 4: in particular, the difficulty of verifying information received from a source with a clear interest and agenda in the conflict; susceptibility to spin; and the danger that the journalist will simply be used to disseminate propaganda. These hazards cannot be entirely removed, whatever approach is taken. After all, they exist when journalists deal with representatives of governments in their own countries, never mind representatives of those governments' enemies. I do, however, think that there are emerging models which will permit us to make the most of the vastly increased access to sources which technological change now gives us, and will continue to give us in the future. I want to make it clear that I am not suggesting that mobile technology and social networking sites will solve all the shortcomings of contemporary conflict reporting. They will not. The picture is more complex than that. As I argued in Chapter 5, technological change has been a burden as well as a boon to journalists covering conflict. I find Robinson *et al.*'s conclusion from their study of the British media reporting the Iraq war convincing: 'our findings regarding the extent of supportive coverage and the continued relevance of the elite driven model caution against any claim that there has been a technology-driven paradigm shift in terms of wartime media-state relations' (2010: 167). In fact, a parallel change in editorial thinking is needed to make the most of the opportunities offered by technological change: Charlie Beckett's 'openness to engage with new sources, perspectives, and narratives' (2008: 150).

There are other challenges too. The political issues are obvious. The approach that led to the silencing of 'terrorists' and their supporters on British airwaves in the 1980s and 1990s would probably still find widespread support among politicians; some support among the public and press; and of course, opponents among the broadcast media. I put forward this suggestion simply in the hope of improving audiences' knowledge – so that they better understand what is happening in their world, especially if it is happening in their name. Then there are huge practical issues – issues of finding the right sources to trust, and getting material from them. Sometimes, of course, the rarest perspectives are those gained only thanks to a reporter's willingness to take risks which many others would find unacceptable. There have always been such reporters and, one fervently hopes, there always will be. The Rory Peck Awards of 2010 gave us two outstanding examples. The finalists for the features award included two journalists who carried out the equivalent of an 'embed', only they accompanied the Taliban rather than the forces occupying the country. The results (Rory Peck Trust, 2010) provide a rare and illuminating view of ordinary Taliban foot soldiers, fighters whom TV viewers are more used to seeing only as distant, indistinct figures, glimpsed as a cameraman ducks to avoid the gunfire. Here they are curious, calculating and sometimes incompetent; not just bomb-layers, but blunderers – human beings, not just shadows. In a related but different way, Wikileaks' WarLogs (Wikileaks, 2010) leaked military documents relating to the campaigns in Afghanistan and Iraq, shedding light on aspects of the occupations of those countries which conventional journalism could not. Now that such large-scale leaks of digital material have started, it is hard to imagine that they will cease: a new factor presenting both challenges and possibilities for the coverage of conflict.

So I would argue that conflict journalists need to draw on as wide a range of sources as possible. This is not a call for a new departure so much as a call for a return to basic, long-established, good journalistic practice. Of course, those sources should not be combatants alone. The theory of 'peace journalism' already promotes the idea of nonviolent responses to conflict. Within this context of drawing on a wider range of sources, Mohammed el-Nawawy and Shawn Powers have also provided this useful view:

> peace journalism authors are not calling for journalists to sanitize their coverage of conflicts, nor focus solely on calls for peace and cooperation. Rather, advocates argue that journalists describe violence in terms of its political, economic and social motivations, rather than a natural or inevitable consequence of otherwise uncontrollable events.
>
> (2010: 67)

My experience as a reporter, however, leads me to disagree with parts of el-Nawawy and Powers's 'typology of a conciliatory media' (ibid.: 69). 'Demonstrating a desire towards solving rather than escalating conflicts' (ibid.: 69), for example, suggests the kind of journalistic engagement that could promote bias in reporting. And much as one might deplore reporting that appears to glorify the waging of war, journalists cannot ignore combatants as sources.

The Gaza model

I have already used the kind of system of sources described above, albeit one set up by my then colleague from the BBC Arabic Service in Gaza, Fayed Abushammala. This 'Gaza model', as I will call it, represents a template for a more effective method of reporting the kind of conflict we have seen in recent years in the Middle East, the North Caucasus and elsewhere: the battles fought by the tracksuited warriors. The Gaza model for conflict reporting is

- collaborative;
- drawn from as many sources as possible – both sides in a conflict indispensable;
- impartial by providing balance *over time*;
- able to use mobile technology and social networking for newsgathering.

Fayed, and the team he had put together in the BBC's bureau in Gaza, had established contacts throughout the territory. These included security officials, medical workers and some people who were just friends, relatives or acquaintances. To me as an outsider, it seemed that such a network could work especially efficiently in Gaza. There, extended family ties, and identities often still proudly defined by the towns and villages in mandate-era Palestine whence many of Gaza's people and their ancestors had fled decades earlier, appeared to have created ideal conditions for the transmission of information. The fact that I did not understand Arabic frustrated my desire to learn more about my host society, but it was also clear that, where no kind of disunity or dissatisfaction could be publicly discussed in case it undermine morale in the face of the enemy, much of what might pass for political debate was limited to private conversation. It was not, for example, considered appropriate to discuss publicly possible corruption in the Palestinian

Authority during the uprising against Israel, the *intifada*. These were issues that I heard spoken of only a little, and in my case, always by English-speaking friends and contacts. But I have no doubt that the conversations whispered behind tea glasses or muttered through exhaled water-pipe smoke contained plenty of such observations and complaints.

There were, then, strong pre-existing links of people knowing each other, or at least of each other, and an established tradition of using these links to carry news and political discussion and speculation. We in the BBC Gaza bureau used the network which Fayed and the others had so efficiently established. When an Israeli military operation began, my colleagues would make sure that I had the latest information as quickly as possible. I was often able to send a first, brief report to London as the story was only just starting to appear on news-agency wires, and sometimes before. I could then add my own observations – on occasion, targets were attacked within a few hundred metres of my apartment or our office – and a comment from the Israeli Army spokesperson's office (although they would frequently say little or nothing during an on-going operation until it was known whether the person or people targeted had been killed).

This was simple news reporting: simple news reporting under intense time pressure and sometimes in danger, but simple news reporting all the same. There was one important characteristic, though, which makes the Gaza model distinct, effective and applicable to the reporting of other conflict. That characteristic is the variety of sources, and the collaborative, collective effort necessary to bring them together to ensure that they were all reflected, in however small a way, in a report which could be as short as thirty-five seconds in duration. One member of the team would gather and filter the information in Arabic as it came in from the network set up by Fayed. I would get information from Israeli sources or, in the cases where British citizens had been shot by the Israelis (there were two of these during my assignment to Gaza: the journalist and cameraman James Miller, and the pro-Palestinian activist Tom Hurndall)[23] from British diplomatic sources. I would then do my best to assemble and edit the information into a report within the time which remained until the next bulletin. Apart from in cases when the Israeli and Palestinian accounts of an incident flatly contradicted each other, and naturally there were more than a few of these, our system worked very well. In such contradictory cases, a reporter just has to accept that, without having been there themselves, they can do no more than relay the two conflicting accounts without offering any conclusion. The longer the system continued working, the more useful I, as the voice and face of the news we were sending to the BBC's English-language outlets, found it as a kind of reference tool, too. The experience gained from reporting many stories of Israeli military activity in Gaza was invaluable in cases where judgement was necessary to try to determine more accurately what might have happened. The more widespread use of such a variety of sources might be a way to address some of the issues identified by the Glasgow Media Group (Philo *et al.*, 2003) concerning the coverage of the Israeli–Palestinian conflict.

Accustomed to access to this type of network, when it came to coverage of the post-invasion situation in Iraq, I experienced a strong sense that we were not getting the full story. Where were the kind of sources which we had come to count on to enable us to report Gaza in such detail? It is my strong feeling now that we should have made a formal suggestion to the BBC that we try to export the Gaza model for use in Iraq. It was too easy, following the capture of Saddam Hussein in December 2003, to see that incident as an unqualified triumph for the United States and its allies. As a public relations event, it was. The timing – a couple of weeks before the New Year – allowed President Bush's administration to end 2003 with an event that the news media were ready and delighted to portray as a big success. The idea that the US could invade Iraq and fail to capture or kill the man they had identified as the reason for that invasion would have been an embarrassment, especially after the then unsuccessful attempts to capture or kill Osama bin Laden.

The public relations triumph was not, of course, the full story. I wrote in Chapter 3 of my realization, on the day when I travelled to the village where Saddam Hussein was captured, that I could not tell the full story because I was not able to talk at any length, or in any detail, to the villagers about their feelings. I look back now at my reports (BBC News, 2003) from then, and the days which followed, and see the disappointment and frustration that some Iraqis expressed. There is an interesting point I now notice with hindsight, too: annoyance that the US Army, and not Iraqis, had captured the former dictator. Should I have placed more emphasis, I wonder, in my reports then on the fact that the US and its allies had only a short time to improve conditions for the people of Iraq before more of those people would turn against those who had presented themselves not as occupiers, but as liberators?

For that is the story which was allowed to escape amid the excitement of Saddam Hussein's capture. We reporters who were there at the time should have made more of the discontent which we sensed then.

We could hardly have gone so far as to predict the insurgency which erupted the following spring. It would have been irresponsible to do so. It would have been irresponsible confidently to predict it, but not irresponsible to warn of it. Such an editorial line would, after all, have been much more responsible than that followed by the *New York Times* and others, for which, as I noted above, they later had to apologize.[24]

So how could that have happened? How could we have stopped the full story getting away? Arriving in Iraq after the invasion, the first priority of the BBC and other media organizations should have been to try to establish a network of the kind built up by Fayed and my other colleagues in Gaza. That way, we could have gathered information from places which became inaccessible as the insurgency continued. Were that to be done today, the increasing presence of computers with internet connections, and mobile phones, could even turn some of those people in the network into actual on-air and on-screen contributors. It is time to challenge the idea that every report should in itself be balanced. This will not be easy, especially in an age when governments seem increasingly concerned about their international media image, as I noted in Chapter 4. Any journalist who has covered the Israeli–Palestinian conflict from both sides knows that the Israelis are especially keen on getting their views across. But there is a precedent. Broadcasters in Britain are subject to legislation which requires them to be impartial in the interests of the electorate. They are not, however, obliged to counter every interview, or even every soundbite, with an immediate, similar response, from an opponent. It is sufficient that such balance is achieved over time (BBC, 2010). The same approach should be adopted in conflict reporting. The BBC's insistence that every story from the Israeli–Palestinian conflict contained a speaker from both sides could just make reporting more difficult. There is no reason why sometimes you could not do an Israeli story one day and a Palestinian one another – and this does occasionally happen. Doing it more frequently could contribute to more comprehensive coverage.

In the last century and a half, we have gone from the era before the professional conflict reporter, through the professional era and into the era where the professional and non-professional co-exist. How can they do so to their full potential? The 'Gaza model' provides the key elements. This approach will not work in every case, but it would have improved the reporting of the Iraq conflict. At the time of writing in August 2011, elements of it are in use in attempts to report the uprisings in Syria. Syria, though, has demonstrated that even in the age of widespread digital technology, when UGC is plentiful, it is still possible, by banning journalists, to stop the outside world from gaining a real impression of what is happening. New technology has, however, meant that this ban is not as effective as it might once have been. Emily Bell (2011) is among those observers who have recognized the role played by National Public Radio's (NPR) Andy Carvin in reporting the Middle East – even though he has done so from the United States, on Twitter. More than a decade ago, and paraphrasing the thoughts of James Carey (1993), Daniel Hallin foresaw a change in the role that the journalist would play in the future, noting that, 'journalists will probably have to shift from conceiving of themselves as, in effect, a representative or stand in for a unitary but inactive public, to a role of facilitating and publicizing public dialogue' (2000: 234–5).

For conflict reporting, though, this is only part of the solution. From my two Russells, James and William Howard, onwards all the way to today, what has characterized good war journalism is being there. This is where the concerns over changes highlighted by Richard Sambrook (2010) come to the fore. Specialist foreign correspondents may be expensive, but, so far at least, no true substitute for their presence and expertise has emerged. It may be that, in the future, the journalist covering conflict will have increasingly to share the screen and the website with those who are not professionals – but it will have to be shared, not ceded. War reporting of this new century, which is unlikely to see an end to the battles of the tracksuited warriors, will need to use contacts which include the equivalents of both Russells, and a nation's enemies, as well as its friends. What will not change is that the best sources will be established by those who know their story, and their region – their 'patch' as journalistic slang has it – as good journalists always have done. In a time of dwindling budgets, and decreasing numbers of foreign bureaux, for western media at least, such expertise is becoming rarer. It must not become extinct, and leave us with reporters who parachute in from time to time to prance around in front of camera, and offer coverage that places self-promotion ahead of information.

Notes

1 I use his own archaic spelling.

2 Throughout, I will use the word audience in the widest possible sense, to reflect that, where once 'readership' might have been more usual or appropriate, the advent of multi-platform journalism, with newspapers' increasing online presence, means that that is no longer the case.

3 This is generally considered to be in the summer of 2000, but there was no formal end to the hostilities, and even though there has been no large-scale Russian military campaign in the North Caucasus since then, at the time of writing (April 2011) the region is increasingly unstable.

4 In the spring of 2011, the posting on Twitter of allegations which had been banned from publication by English court injunction led to a debate in Britain on technology, the media and privacy.

5 The second *intifada*, or Palestinian uprising against Israel, had begun in September 2000. March 2003 was an especially intense period of Israeli military activity in the Gaza Strip and on the West Bank.

6 A 1917 expression of support by the British government for the idea of a Jewish homeland.

7 Stalin's decision to deport the Chechens during the Second World War on the grounds that they might not be sufficiently loyal to the Soviet state, and the attack on Chechnya from December 1994 onwards, were usually presented as evidence for this.

8 A BBC current affairs programme.

9 The location of the main Russian military base in Chechnya.

10 The principal town in the Russian region of North Ossetia, bordering Chechnya, but removed from the front line.

11 According to the Ofcom broadcasting code, context includes (but is not limited to):

- the editorial content of the programme, programmes or series;
- the service on which the material is broadcast;
- the time of broadcast;
- what other programmes are scheduled before and after the programme or programmes concerned;
- the degree of harm or offence likely to be caused by the inclusion of any particular sort of material in programmes generally or programmes of a particular description;

- the likely size and composition of the potential audience and likely expectation of the audience;
- the extent to which the nature of the content can be brought to the attention of the potential audience for example by giving information; and
- the effect of the material on viewers or listeners who may come across it unawares.

(Ofcom, 2010)

12   A revolutionary.
13   Irregular troops loyal to the Russian tsar, or emperor.
14   The main town in South Ossetia.
15   The report of the Independent International Fact-Finding Mission on the Conflict in Georgia. This report was not published until September 2009, so its findings were of no help to Russia at this early stage of the information war.
16   As Roxburgh explained during the interview, these included the belief that a favourable editorial could simply be bought.
17   There is now a South Ossetian website http://www.osetinfo.ru/spisok (accessed 20 May 2011), which puts the number killed at 365. This figure, though, refers to deaths between 7 and 12 August 2008, not during the initial assault alone and, in any case, is substantially lower than the original figure.
18   Television footage of the Georgian president, Mikheil Saakashvili chewing his tie hardly helped.
19   Sontag seems to make the same error as Tumber and Webster regarding the status of Chechnya.
20   In 1994, at the height of the massacres in Rwanda, I heard one news editor telling a colleague, 'At the end of the day, it's only foreigners killing each other.'
21   Israel Defense Forces (the Israeli Army).
22   Arabic speakers may point out the inconsistent transliteration of these names. I have chosen the transliterations that these journalists themselves use, and that appear as their BBC bylines.
23   James Miller was shot and killed on 2 May 2003. Tom Hurndall was shot on 11 April 2003. He died of his wounds on 6 January 2004.
24   I would not want to give the impression that the errors admitted by the *New York Times* should detract from some outstanding reporting of the conflict itself, where their correspondents worked very hard to reflect multiple voices and views. Examples include the following (all accessed 20 May 2011):

- *Violence Surges through Central and Northern Iraq*, available online at http://www.nytimes.com/2004/11/20/international/middleeast/20cnd-iraq.html?pagewanted=1&fta=y;
- *In Falluja, Young Marines Saw the Savagery of an Urban War*, available

online at http://www.nytimes.com/2004/11/21/international/middle
east/21battle.html?scp=1&sq=filkins%20fallujah%20november%
202004&st=cse;

- *For One Family in Falluja, a Simple Drive Turns Deadly*, available online at
http://www.nytimes.com/2004/11/20/international/middleeast/
20family.html?adxnnl=1&fta=y&adxnnlx=1296310000-m0Q6TmkwIJ
3cIIgHXuETfg.

References

Abou Alouf, Rusdhi (2009a) *Missiles Greet Gaza at New Year*, available online at http://news.bbc.co.uk/1/hi/world/middle_east/7807311.stm (accessed 20 December 2010).

Abou Alouf, Rushdi (2009b) *Inside Gaza*, available online at http:// news. bbc. co.uk/1/hi/world/middle_east/7833026.stm (accessed 20 December 2010).

Abu Qammar, Hamada (2009) *Fear for Homes amid Gaza Danger*, available online at http://news.bbc.co.uk/1/hi/world/middle_east/7812168.stm (accessed 20 December 2010).

Allan, Stuart and Zelizer, Barbie (eds) (2004) *Reporting War: Journalism in Wartime* (Abingdon: Routledge).

Arlidge, John (2011) 'The Eye of the Storm', *Sunday Times Magazine*, 13 March 2011, pp. 22–30.

Baudelaire, Charles (1968) 'The Painter of Modern Life', *Oeuvres Complètes* (Paris: Éditions du Seuil).

Baudrillard, Jean (2009) *The Gulf War Did Not Take Place*, translated and with an introduction by Paul Patton (Sydney: Power Publications).

BBC Editorial Guidelines (2010a) *Conflicts of Interest Introduction*, available online at http://www.bbc.co.uk/guidelines/editorialguidelines/page/guidance-conflicts-introduction (accessed 2 May 2011).

BBC Editorial Guidelines (2010b) *Impartiality over Time*, available online at http:// www.bbc.co.uk/guidelines/editorialguidelines/page/guideliens-impartiality-series-time/ (accessed 10 August 2011).

BBC Editorial Guidelines (2010c) *Section 4 Impartiality Introduction*, available online at http://www.bbc.co.uk/editorialguidelines/page/guidelines-impartiality-introduction (accessed 10 August 2011).

BBC Editorial Guidelines (2010d) *Section 5 Harm and Offence*, available online at http://www.bbc.co.uk/guidelines/editorialguidelines/page/guidelines-harm-violence (accessed 2 May 2011).

BBC Editorial Guidelines *Section 11* (2010e) *War, Terror and Emergencies*, available online at http://www.bbc.co.uk/guidelines/editorialguidelines/page/guide-lines-war-principles (accessed 2 May 2011).

BBC News (2003) *Reporters' Log: Saddam's Capture*, available online at http://news.bbc.co.uk/1/hi/world/middle_east/3317945.stm (accessed 20 May 2011).

BBC News (2008a) *A Prime Minister, a Party and a Ban*, available online at http://news.bbc.co.uk/1/hi/northern_ireland/7674184.stm (accessed 20 May 2011).

BBC News (2008b) *No Charges over Reporter's Death*, available online at http://news.bbc.co.uk/1/hi/uk/7528749.stm (accessed 29 April 2011).

BBC News (2009) *Israel Troops Admit Gaza Abuses*, available online at http://news.bbc.co.uk/1/hi/world/middle_east/7952603.stm (accessed 20 December 2010).

BBC News (2011) *Gaza Unemployment Levels 'among Worst in World'*, available online at http://www.bbc.co.uk/news/world-middle-east-13758003 (accessed 25 June 2011).

BBC Trust (2007) *From Seesaw to Wagon Wheel: Safeguarding Impartiality in the 21st Century*, available online at http://news.bbc.co.uk/1/shared/bsp/hi/pdfs/18_06_07impartialitybbc.pdf (accessed 10 August 2011).

BBC World Service (2010) *Gaza One Year On*, available online at http://www.bbc.co.uk/worldservice/news/2009/12/091222_palestinian_doctor_wt_sl.shtml (accessed 20 May 2011).

Beckett, Charlie (2008) *Supermedia* (Oxford: Blackwell).

Bell, Emily (2011) 'In the Absence of Public Media Funding, the US Has Outsourced Its National Voice', *Guardian* website, available online at http://www.guardian.co.uk/media/organgrinder/2011/feb/25/public-media-funding-america?INTCMP=SRCH (accessed 20 June 2011).

Bell, Martin (1995) *In Harm's Way: Reflections of a War Zone Thug* (London: Hamish Hamilton).

Bell, Melissa (2011) 'Egypt Protests "Day of Departure" Day Eleven', *Washington Post* website, available online at http://voices.washingtonpost.com/blog-post/2011/02/egypt_protests_ day_eleven.html (accessed 16 June 2011).

Bolton, Roger (1990) *Death on the Rock and Other Stories* (London: W. H. Allen).

Briggs, Asa (1985) *The BBC: The First Fifty Years* (Oxford: Oxford University Press).

Brown, Ben (2003) 'Basra – The Second City Falls', in Beck, S. and Downing, M. (eds), *The Battle for Iraq* (London: BBC Worldwide), pp. 29–32.

Brown, Robin (2003) 'Spinning the War: Political Communications, Information Operations, and Public Diplomacy in the War on Terrorism', in Thussu, D. K. and Freedman, D. (eds), *War and the Media* (London: Sage), pp. 87–100.

Cameron, David (2008) 'We Must Make Moscow Pay for This Blow against democracy', *Sunday Times*, 17 August, available online at http://www.timesonline.co.uk/tol/news/world/europe/article4547747.ece (accessed 10 May 2011).

Carey, James (1993) 'The Mass Media and Democracy: Between the Modern and the Postmodern', *Journal of International Affairs* vol. 47 no.1, pp. 1–21.

Carruthers, Susan (2000) *The Media at War* (Basingstoke: Palgrave).

Carruthers, Susan (2011) *The Media at War*, 2nd edn (Basingstoke: Palgrave).

Chambers, Roland (2009).*The Last Englishman: The Double Life of Arthur Ransome* (London: Faber and Faber.)

CNN (2009) *Israel Explains Gaza Media Restriction*, available online at http://edition.cnn.com/2009/WORLD/meast/01/14/israel.gaza.media.restrictions/index.html?iref=allsearch (accessed 20 May 2011).

Committee to Protect Journalists (2011) *861 Journalists Killed since 1992*, available online at http://www.cpj.org/killed/ (accessed 28 April 2011).

Curtis, Liz (1998) *Ireland: the Propaganda War* (Belfast: Sasta)

Dart Center for Journalism and Trauma (2011) http://dartcenter.org/. (accessed 9 August 2011).

Davies, Nick (2008) *Flat Earth News: An Award-winning Reporter Exposes Falsehood, Distortion, and Propaganda in the Global Media* (London: Chatto & Windus).

Davis, Aeron (2002) *Public Relations Democracy: Public Relations, Politics, and the Mass Media in Britain* (Manchester: Manchester University Press).

Di Giovanni, Janine (2006) *The Place at the End of the World. Essays from the Edge.* (London, Bloomsbury).

Feinstein, Anthony (2006) *Journalists under Fire: The Psychological Hazards of Covering War* (Baltimore, MD: Johns Hopkins University Press).

Figes, Orlando (2010) *Crimea: The Last Crusade* (London: Allen Lane).

Franklin, Bob and Carlson, Matt (2011) (eds), *Journalists, Sources and Credibility: New Perspectives* (Abingdon: Routledge).

Gardiner, Sam (2003) 'Truth from These Podia', available online at http://www.flatearthnews.net/files/Truth%20from%20These%20Podia.pdf (accessed 25 January 2011).

Gellhorn, Martha (1998) *The Face of War* (London: Granta).

Gellner, Ernest (1996) *Conditions of Liberty: Civil Society and Its Rivals* (London: Penguin).

Greene, Graham (2001) *The Quiet American* (London: Vintage Classics).

Grossman, Vassily (2006) *A Writer at War: Vassily Grossman with the Red Army 1941–1945*, edited and translated by A. Beevor and L. Vinogradova (London: Pimlico).

Hallin, Daniel (1989) *The 'Uncensored War': The Media and Vietnam* (London: University of California Press).

Hallin, Daniel (2000) 'Commercialism and Professionalism in the American News Media', in Curran, J. and Gurevitch, M. (eds), *Mass Media and Society* (London: Arnold), pp. 218–37.

Herman, Edward S. and Chomsky, Noam (1994) *Manufacturing Consent* (London: Vintage).

Herr, Michael (1977) *Dispatches* (London: Macmillan).

Human Rights Watch (2009) *Up in Flames: Humanitarian Law Violations and Civilian Victims in the Conflict over South Ossetia* (New York: Human Rights Watch).

Independent International Fact-Finding Mission on the Conflict in Georgia (2009) *Report*, available online at http://www.ceiig.ch/Index.html (accessed 10 May 2011).

International Federation of Journalists (2009) *The End of a Deadly Decade*, available online at http://www.ifj.org/assets/docs/059/046/c93b13b-7a4a82e.pdf (accessed 28 April 2011).

Jerusalem Post (2010) *IDF Warns Troops: Enemies, Terrorists Can Use Facebook*, available online at http://www.jpost.com/Defense/Article.aspx?id=201058 (accessed 15 January 2011)

Al-Khairalla, Musab and Carey, Nick (2011) *Tripoli Activists Plot Revolt without Facebook*, Reuters website available online at http://uk.reuters.com/article/2011/06/24/libya-tripoli-networks-idUKLDE75M0TJ20110624 (accessed 25 June 2011).

Knightley, Phillip (1989) *The First Casualty* (London: Pan).

Lichtenberg, Judith (2000) 'In Defence of Objectivity Revisited', in Curran, J. and Gurevitch, M. (eds) *Mass Media and Society* (London: Arnold), pp. 238–54.

Loyd, Anthony (2000) *My War Gone By, I Miss It So* (London: Anchor).

Maass, Peter (2011) *The Toppling: How the Media Inflated a Minor Moment in a Long War*, available online at http://www.newyorker.com/reporting/2011/01/10/110110fa_fact_maass (accessed 10 February 2011).

McCrum, Robert (2011) 'Lessons Learned from a Gay Girl in Damascus', *Guardian* website, available online at http://www.guardian.co.uk/books/booksblog/2011/jun/15/lessons-learned-gay-girl-damascus?INTCMP=SRCH. (accessed 25 June 2011).

McCullin, Don (1992) *Unreasonable Behaviour* (London: Vintage).

Miller, David (ed.) (2004) *Tell Me Lies: Propaganda Media Distortion in the Attack on Iraq* (London: Pluto).

Ministry of Foreign Affairs of the Russian Federation (2008) *Dmitry Medvedev Instructed the Russian Federation Prosecutor General's Office Committee of Inquiry to Document Crimes Committed in South Ossetia in Order to Prosecute the Perpetrators*, available online at http://www.mid.ru/brp_4.nsf/0/27B12D7 8E53C9B0AC3257523003F9D54 (accessed 20 May 2011).

Moorcraft, Paul and Taylor, Philip (2008) *Shooting the Messenger: The Political Impact of War Reporting* (Dulles, WA: Potomac).

Morozov, Evgeny (2011) *Net Delusion: The Dark Side of Internet Freedom* (New York: PublicAffairs).

Morrison, David and Tumber, Howard (1988) *Journalists at War: The Dynamics of News Reporting during the Falklands Conflict* (London: Sage).

Mosco, Vincent (2009) *The Political Economy of Communication* (London: Sage).

Moynihan, Michael (1994) *War Correspondent* (Barnsley: Pen & Sword).

el-Nawawy, Mohammed and Powers, Shawn (2010) 'Al-Jazeera English: A Conciliatory Medium in a Conflict-driven Environment?', *Global Media and Communication* vol 6 no. 1, pp. 61–84.

New York Times, (2004) *From the Editors*, available online at http://www.nytimes.com/2004/05/26/international/middleeast/26FTE_NOTE.html (accessed 11 January 2011).

Ofcom (2010) 'In Breach. News. Al Jazeera, 9 February 2010, 21:04', *Ofcom Broadcast Bulletin* no. 156, 26 April 2010, available online at http://stakeholders.ofcom.org.uk/binaries/enforcement/broadcast-bulletins/obb156/Issue156.pdf. (accessed 16 June 2011).

Ofcom (2011) The Ofcom Broadcasting Code, Section 2, 'Harm and Offence', available online at http://stakeholders.ofcom.org.uk/broadcasting/broadcast-codes/broadcast-code/harmoffence/. (accessed 16 June 2011).

Paterson, Chris and Sreberny, Annabelle (2004) *International News in the Twenty-first Century* (Eastleigh: John Libbey Publishing for the University of Luton Press).

Pax, Salam (2003) http://salampax.wordpress.com/2003/01/ (accessed 11 January 2011).

Peace Journalism (2011) http://www.peacejournalism.org/Welcome.html (accessed 29 January 2011).

Pearse, Damian and Weaver, Matthew (2009) 'Timeline: The Death of Ian Tomlinson', *Guardian*, available online at http://www.guardian.co.uk/uk/2009/may/15/ian-tomlinson-death-g20 (accessed 16 May 2011).

Philo, Greg (2004) 'The Mass Production of Ignorance: News Content and Audience', in Paterson, C. and Sreberny, A. (eds), *International News in the Twenty-first Century* (Eastleigh: John Libbey Publishing for the University of Luton Press), pp. 199–224.

Philo, Greg, Gilmour, Alison, Gilmour, Maureen, Rust, Susanna, Gaskell, Etta, West, Lucy (Glasgow University Media Group) (2003) 'The Israeli–Palestinian Conflict: TV News and Public Understanding', in Thussu, D. K. and Freedman, D. (eds), *War and the Media* (London: Sage), pp. 133–48.

Plunkett, John and Halliday, Josh (2011) 'Al-Jazeera's Coverage of Egypt Protests May Hasten Revolution in World News', *Guardian*, 7 February 2011, available online at http://www.guardian.co.uk/media/2011/feb/07/al-jazeera-television-egypt-protests?INTCMP=SRCH (accessed 17 February 2011).

Politkovskaya, Anna (2003) *A Small Corner of Hell: Dispatches from Chechnya*, translated by A. Burry and T. Tulchinsky (London: University of Chicago Press).

Preston, Jennifer (2011) 'Seeking to Disrupt Protesters, Syria Cracks Down on Social Media', *New York Times*, available online at http://www.nytimes.com/2011/05/23/world/middleeast/23facebook.html (accessed 27 July 2011).

Reed, John (1977) *Ten Days That Shook the World* (London: Penguin).

Reporters without Borders (2009) *Invisible Injuries That Threaten the Lives of Journalists*, available online at http://en.rsf.org/invisible-injuries-that-threaten-10-06-2009,33366.html (accessed 9 August 2011).

Reporters without Borders (2011) *2011: 18 Journalists Killed*, available online at http://en.rsf.org/press-freedom-barometer-journalists-killed.html?annee=2011 (accessed 28 April 2011).

Robinson, Piers (2004) 'Researching US Media–State Relations and 21st Century Wars', in Allan, S. and Zelizer, B. (eds), *Reporting War: Journalism in Wartime* (Abingdon: Routledge), pp. 96–112.

Robinson, Piers, Goddard, Peter, Parry, Katy, Murray, Craig with Taylor, Philip M. (2010) *Pockets of Resistance: British News Media, War, and Theory in the 2003 Invasion of Iraq* (Manchester: Manchester University Press).

Rodgers, James (2003) *Iraq Freedom and Poverty Tug-of-war*, available online at http://news.bbc.co.uk/1/hi/world/middle_east/3330409.stm (first published 18 December 2003, accessed 10 February 2011).

Rodgers, James (2008a) *Grim Reminders as Russian Troops Leave*, available online at http://news.bbc.co.uk/1/hi/world/europe/7659556.stm (first published 8 October 2008, accessed 16 May 2011).

Rodgers, James (2008b) *Russian Troops Withdraw*, available online at http://news.bbc.co.uk/1/hi/world/europe/7660232.stm (first broadcast 8 October 2008, accessed 16 May 2011).

Rodgers, James (writer and presenter) and Edmonds, David (producer) (2008) *The PR Battle for the Caucasus*, BBC World Service, available online at http://www.bbc.co.uk/worldservice/documentaries/2008/10/081029_caucases_doc.shtml (first broadcast November 2008, accessed 10 May 2011).

Rory Peck Trust, (2010) http://www.rorypecktrust.org/page/3190/Features+Finalists+2010 (accessed 15 January 2011).

Russell, William Howard (2008) *Despatches from the Crimea* (London: Frontline).

Sambrook, Richard (2010) 'Are Foreign Correspondents Redundant?', available online at http://reutersinstitute.politics.ox.ac.uk/publications/risj-challenges/are-foreign-correspondents-redundant.html (accessed 14 April 2011).

Schneider, Thomas (2011) 'Narrating the War in Pictures: German Photo Books on World War I and the Construction of Pictorial War Narrations', *Journal of War and Culture Studies* vol. 4 no. 1 pp. 31–50.

Schudson, Michael (2000) 'The Sociology of News Production Revisited (Again)', in Curran, J. and Gurevitch, M. (eds) *Mass Media and Society* (London: Arnold), pp. 175–200.

Seaton, Jean (2003) 'Understanding Not Empathy', in Thussu, D. K. and Freedman D. (eds), *War and the Media* (London: Sage), pp. 45–54.

Seib, Philip (2008) *The Al Jazeera Effect: How the New Global Media Are Reshaping World Politics* (Dulles, WA: Potomac).

Shirky, Clay (2008) *Here Comes Everybody* (London: Penguin).

Sontag, Susan (2003) *Regarding the Pain of Others* (London: Penguin).

Sonwalkar, Prasun (2004) 'Out of Sight, out of Mind?: The Non-reporting of Small Wars and Insurgencies', in Allan, S. and Zelizer, B. (eds), *Reporting War: Journalism in Wartime* (Abingdon: Routledge).

Sreberny, A. (2002) 'Trauma Talk: Reconfiguring the Inside and Outside', in Zelizer, B. and Allan, S. (eds) *Journalism after September 11th* (London: Routledge) pp, 220–34.

Stewart, Rebecca (2011) *Sec. Gates: U.S. Engaged in 'Preliminary' Peace Talks with the Taliban* (CNN), available online at http://politicalticker.blogs.cnn.com/2011/06/19/sec-gates-u-s-engaged-in-preliminary-peace-talks-with-the-taliban/?iref=allsearch (accessed 20 June 2011).

Streatfeild, Richard (2011) Interview with the author, London, 6 January.

Streatfeild, Richard *Afghan Diary Frontline*, available online at http://www.bbc.co.uk/search/news/?q=streatfeild (accessed 12 February 2011).

Thomson, Alex (1992) *Smokescreen: The Media, the Censors, the Gulf* (Tunbridge Wells: Laburnham and Spellmount).

Thussu, Daya Kishan (2003) 'Live TV and Bloodless Deaths: War, Infotainment and 24/7 News', in Thussu D. K. and Freedman, D. (eds) (2003) *War and the Media* (London Sage), pp. 117–32.

Thussu, Daya Kishan and Freedman, Des (eds) (2003) *War and the Media* (London: Sage).

Tumber, Howard (2003) 'Reporting under Fire: The Physical Safety and Emotional Welfare of Journalists', in Zelizer, B. and Allan, S. (eds), *Journalism after September 11* (London: Routledge).

Tumber, Howard and Palmer, Jerry (2004) *The Media at War: The Iraq Crisis* (London: Sage).

Tumber, Howard and Prentoulis, Maria (2003) 'Journalists under Fire: Subcultures, Objectivity and Emotional Literacy', in Thussu, D. K. and Freedman, D. (eds) *War and the Media* (London: Sage) pp. 215–31.

Tumber, Howard and Webster, Frank (2006) *Journalists under Fire: Information War and Journalistic Practices* (London: Sage).

Waisbord, Silvio (2002) 'Journalism, Risk, and Patriotism', in Zelizer, B. and Allan, S. (eds), *Journalism after September 11* (London: Routledge), pp. 201–19.

Waugh, Evelyn (1938) *Scoop* (London: Penguin).

Wells, Matt (2011) 'How Live Blogging Has Transformed Journalism', *Guardian*, 28 March 2011, available online at http://www.guardian.co.uk/media/2011/mar/28/live-blogging-transforms-journalism?INTCMP=SRCH (accessed 16 June 2011).

Wikileaks (2010) *WarLogs*, available online at http://wikileaks.ch/iraq/diarydig/ (accessed 11 August 2011).

Williams, Jon (2009) *Covering Gaza*, available online at http://www.bbc.co.uk/blogs/theeditors/2009/01/covering_gaza.html (accessed 20 May 2011).

Wood, Paul (2009) *Analysis: Operation Miscast Lead?*, available online at http://news.bbc.co.uk/1/hi/world/middle_east/7940624.stm. (accessed 20 May 2011).

Wright, Evan (2009) *Generation Kill* (London: Corgi).

ynet (2010) *Hamas Warned against Visitng* (sic) *Targeted Operative's Facebook Page* http://www.ynetnews.com/articles/0,7340,L-3967193,00.html (accessed 20 May 2011).

Zelizer, Barbie and Allan, Stuart (eds) (2002) *Journalism after September 11* (London: Routledge).

Index

Abou Alouf, Rushdi, 110–13, 115
Abu Qammar, Hamada, 110–15
Abushammala, Fayed, 49, 113, 134
access, xi, 3, 6, 7, 10, 15, 19, 20, 24, 28, 29, 30, 31, 33, 34, 37–43, 45, 49, 51, 61–3, 71, 77, 80, 85, 87, 98, 100, 125, 130, 131, 132, 136
accreditation, 20, 47
Afghanistan, 5, 8, 109, 110, 116, 126, 130, 133
AFP, 131
Africa, 2, 86, 87, 95, 96
agencies, 49, 70, 71, 131
AJE, 59
Al-Jazeera, 59, 85, 87, 88, 97
Al Rasheed (hotel), xii
Arab, 59, 81, 86, 87, 101, 106, 111, 123, 130
Arabic, 49, 113, 134, 135, 140
ARD, xi
Armenia, 1
As-Shifa (hospital, Gaza), 112, 113

Baghdad, xii, xiii, 17, 23, 40, 60, 61, 63, 99, 125
Bahrain, 2
Balfour Declaration, 52
Balkans, xi, 2
Basra, 31, 74, 88
BBC, viii, x, 1, 2, 4, 5, 7, 14, 18, 23, 32, 37, 41, 49, 53, 54, 56, 58, 59, 61, 68, 70, 72, 75, 78, 81, 87, 88, 89, 91, 97, 100, 105, 106, 110–13, 115, 122, 125–31, 134–7, 139, 140
Beckett, Charlie, 22, 85, 123, 125
Beijing, 68
Belgravia, 130
Bell, Emily, 138
Bell, Martin, 7, 18–20, 54, 55, 65, 88, 89
Bell, Melissa, 87
bias, 44, 64, 117, 134
bin Laden, Osama, 123, 136
Blair, Tony, 54, 129
Bosnia, 18–20, 55, 118
Bremmer, Paul, 60

Britain, iv, 5, 10, 12, 14, 18, 58, 73, 80, 126, 137, 139
broadcasting, 4, 5, 14, 17, 18, 23, 24, 25, 27, 54, 58, 59, 60, 62, 71, 78, 81, 87, 88, 91, 94, 96, 99, 112, 113, 126, 128, 131, 133, 137, 139
Brown, Ben, 31
Brown, Robin, 67, 73–74, 77
Brussels, 1, 26, 69, 70, 71, 72, 75, 94
budgets, 69, 88, 95, 138
Bush, George W., 54, 67, 71, 122, 124

cameras, 4, 23, 60, 90–2, 94, 105, 113, 131, 138
Cameron, David, 76
Carey, James, 138
Carey, Nick, 87
Carlson, Matt, 125
Carruthers, Susan, 13–16, 24, 29, 35, 36, 43, 48, 49, 52, 54, 67, 74, 85, 96, 106, 109, 119, 122
Carvin, Andy, 138
Caucasus, 2, 7, 34, 43, 49, 56–7, 68, 72, 79, 92, 93, 102, 134, 139
censorship, 13–14, 36, 38, 43, 126
Chalabi, Ahmad, 124
Chechnya, 13, 32–4, 53, 55, 57, 64–5, 79–80, 81, 83, 92, 119, 139, 140
checkpoints, xi, 34
Chicherov, Anton, 93
Chomsky, Noam, 15–16, 66
civilians, xii, 1, 5, 10, 19, 23, 25, 29, 31–2, 34, 41, 46, 57–60, 62–3, 78–81, 93, 94, 97, 104, 110–12, 121
CNM (Conflict News Management), 83
CNN (Cable News Network), 18, 72, 83, 110, 124
Cold War, x, 1, 2, 4, 9, 10, 18, 19, 27, 55, 60, 66, 67, 75, 80, 123
Communism, 19, 67, 80
Communist, ix, 20, 63, 67
conflict, vii, x, 1–25, 27–30, 32, 33, 35, 38–40, 42, 43–5, 47–9, 52–5, 57–9, 62–75, 77–84, 86, 88–90, 94, 95–9, 103, 104, 105–13, 116–20, 123, 126, 128–38, 140

Congo, 8, 81
Conservative, 76, 130
consultants, 7, 51, 68, 75, 94
context, 31, 37, 52, 53, 56, 58, 64–5, 82,
    96, 98, 116, 133, 139
Cossacks, 63
Couso, Jose, 40
CPA (Coalition Provisional Authority in
    Iraq), 60
Crimea, 9–10, 12, 28, 127
Czechoslovakia, ix

danger, 12, 21, 28, 30, 34, 38–9, 47,
    58–9, 89, 96, 111, 115–17, 119,
    130, 132, 135
Darfur, 8, 81
Davies, Nick, 51, 73–4, 125
Davis, Aeron, 51
deadlines, 6, 22, 31, 61, 62, 80, 84, 89,
    92, 121
despotism, x
dictatorship, 72, 136
diplomacy, 2, 10, 16, 68, 73, 81, 99, 135
Druce, Ian, 90
Dubcek, Alexander, ix

economics, 8
Edinburgh, xii
Edmonds, David, 7, 68
Egypt, 2, 87, 90
el-Nawawy, Mohammed, 133–4
embedding, 23, 29–31, 33, 36–8, 42–3,
    45, 62, 106, 110
espionage, 44
ethics, 10, 14, 31, 41, 85, 115
Euphrates, xii
Europe, iv, ix, x, 1, 2, 12–14, 19, 111
Evans, Richard, 8

Facebook, 26, 28, 85–7, 130
Falklands, 3, 10, 29, 33, 35
Fallujah, 125
Feinstein, Anthony, 103–4
Figes, Orlando, 10
Fisk, Robert, 53–4
Floto, Jo, 106
France, 10, 12, 26, 69, 131
Franklin, Bob, 125
freedom, x, 13, 24, 69, 103, 112
FSB, 34

G20, 86
G8, 69
Gardiner, Sam, 73–4

Gaza, viii, 1, 7, 22, 23, 40–4, 49–53,
    59–60, 63, 79, 81, 83, 90, 97, 101,
    103, 106, 109, 110–22, 130,
    134–7, 139
Gellhorn, Martha, x
Gellner, Ernest, x
Georgia, 7, 19, 20, 25, 44, 49, 66, 68–74,
    76, 92–3, 140
Glasgow University Media Group, 53,
    136
globalization, 8, 82
GMTV, 130
Gori, 72–4, 76
governments, vii, x, 5, 13, 15–17, 31–4,
    40, 43, 44, 51, 57, 64, 66–9, 71,
    73, 75–7, 79, 81–4, 87, 100, 115,
    122, 124, 129–32, 137, 139
GPlus, 69, 75
Graham, Philip, 6, 19, 46
Greene, Graham, 19, 46
Grossman, Vassily, viii, 7, 14–15, 22,
    38–9, 45, 109
Grozny, 34–5, 63, 116
Guardian (newspaper), 87, 125
Gulf, xii, xiii, 16, 18, 39, 62, 77

Hallin, Daniel, 15–16, 67, 138
Hamas, 42, 85, 111, 113–14
Hanoi, 131
Havel, Vaclav, ix
hazards, 125, 132
Heriot-Watt, xii
Herman, Edward, 15–16, 20, 66
Herr, Michael, 6, 84, 91, 100, 102, 117
Hetherington, Tim, 39
history, vii, viii, xiii, 1, 2, 5–9, 10–11,
    13, 15, 17, 19, 21, 23, 25, 27, 52,
    53, 63, 126–7
Hondros, Chris, 39
hostages, 80
Hunt, James, 70, 72, 75
Hurndall, Tom, 135, 140
Hussein, Saddam, xii, xiii, 7, 17, 23, 32,
    60, 61, 62, 64–5, 100, 119, 121–4,
    136
IDF (Israel Defense Forces – the Israeli
    Army), 140
IFJ (International Federation of
    Journalists), 40
impartiality, 11, 47–8, 121–2, 126, 130,
    132, 134, 137
Independent, 53, 118, 140
India, 82
infotainment, 59

Ingushetia, 80
instant-messaging, 85
insurgency, 62, 100, 132, 137
insurgents, 2, 132
Internationale, 63
internet, 5, 21, 23, 27, 46, 84–7, 93, 99,
    100, 129–30, 137
intervention, 80, 118
interviewees, 5, 34
interviews, 39, 71, 75, 77, 90, 91, 93, 94,
    113, 121, 127, 131, 137, 140
intifada, 7, 90, 135, 139
involvement, vii, 10, 19–20, 24, 102–3,
    105–6, 107, 109, 111, 113, 115,
    117, 119, 129
IRA (Irish Republican Army), 5
Iran, 54
Iraq, xi, xii, xiii, 5, 9, 15, 17–18, 22–4,
    27, 29, 30–1, 33, 35, 37, 39–40,
    54, 60–1, 66, 74, 77, 88, 95,
    99–100, 106, 109–10, 116, 121–6,
    129, 131–3, 136–7, 140
Ireland, 131
Islamic fundamentalists, 108
Israel, 23, 40, 44, 50, 52, 54, 80–1, 85,
    97, 98, 99, 109–11, 122, 135, 139
Israeli, 23, 40–3, 49–53, 59, 79–81, 90,
    97, 99, 103, 110–17, 119, 130,
    135–7, 139–40
ITN (Independent Television News), 32

Jabalya, 41–2
Jerusalem, 41–2, 51, 81, 130
Jewish, 14–15, 110, 139
jingoism, 119, 125
journalism, vii, viii, x, xi, xiii, 2–10, 13,
    18–19, 28, 47–8, 51–2, 54–6, 60,
    62, 65–7, 73, 77–8, 83–6, 88,
    99–100, 104, 106, 108–10, 114,
    118–20, 123, 125–6, 132–3, 138–9
journalists, viii, xi, xii, xiii, xiv, 1–10,
    14–16, 19–26, 28–33, 35–6,
    39–40, 42–54, 58, 60–2, 64–5,
    68–9, 71–82, 84, 89, 91, 94,
    97–110, 112–24, 126–8, 130–5,
    137–8, 140
JUSPAO (Joint United States Public
    Affairs Office), 77

Ketchum, 69
KGB, 34, 85
kidnapping, 80
Klimov, Andrei, 70–1
Knightley, Phillip, 13, 29, 127–9

Korea, x
Kremlin, 57, 71, 75
Kuwait, xi, xii, xiii, 17, 122

Labour, 129
language, 8, 20, 22, 28, 43, 59, 95, 111,
    136
Lavrov, Sergei, 71
Lebanon, 54
Lenin, Vladimir Ilyich, 63
Libya, 2, 39
Lichtenberg, Judith, 57, 64
Lloyd, Terry, 32
London, iv, viii, xii, 1, 3, 8, 46, 47, 52,
    75–7, 81, 87, 89, 93, 103, 115–16,
    121, 127, 131, 135

Madrid, 115
management, 67, 73, 76–7, 84, 88
Manhattan, 82, 107
Manufacturing Consent, 15, 66
marines, xi, xii, 32, 35, 36, 37, 140
media, xiii, 3–5, 9–10, 15–17, 21, 23–5,
    31, 35–6, 39, 40, 47, 53, 58, 62,
    67–9, 71, 73–81, 84–7, 89, 91, 94,
    96, 98–9, 101, 108–11, 113, 120,
    122–5, 127, 129, 130, 132–3,
    136–8
Medvedev, Dmitry, 71
mercenaries, 70–1
mercenary, 83, 105
Merkusheva, Daria, 93
Mexico, 8
microblogging, 5
Miller, David, 122
Miller, James, 40, 90, 135, 140
Miller, Judith, 48
misinformation, 124
Misrata, 63, 116
MOD (Ministry of Defence), 127–9
Moorcraft, Paul, 81
Morozov, Evgeny, 85, 130
Morrison, David, 3, 10, 15, 29, 35, 47–8,
    117
Mosco, Vincent, 24
Moscow, viii, x, 1, 13, 19–20, 32–4, 57,
    68, 70, 71, 75, 80, 89
motivation, 53, 103–5, 133
Moynihan, Michael, 12
Mozdok, 33, 102
Mullah Omar, 108
multimedia, 101
multi-platform, vii, 12, 84–5, 87, 89, 91,
    93, 95, 97, 99, 101, 139

Mumbai, 115
Muscovite, 11

Nasariyah, xii
NATO (North Atlantic Treaty
    Organization), 44, 70
Nazi, 14, 109
neo-conservative, 125
Nerac, Fred, 32
New York Times, 9, 10, 17, 56, 76, 124–5,
    130, 137, 140
newsgathering, 3, 4, 7, 9, 10, 12, 18, 24,
    80, 86, 89, 91, 94, 95, 101, 112,
    134
newspapers, ix, 4, 5, 10, 11, 13–14, 21,
    25, 27, 63, 75, 82, 87–8, 95–6,
    123–4, 127–9
Nicholson, Michael, 118
non-combatants, 16, 49
NPR (National Public Radio), 138
Nuseirat, 111, 114

objectivity, vii, 7, 10, 13–14, 19–20, 22,
    24, 44, 46–9, 51, 53–65, 67, 72,
    106–7, 121,
Ofcom, 58, 59, 139, 140
officer-journalist, 5
Olympic Games, 68, 70
Ossetia, 7, 33, 44, 68, 69, 72, 75–8, 83,
    92, 101, 139–40

Palestine, 40, 111, 134
Palestinian journalists, 23, 50, 97–8,
    109–15, 119
Palmer, Jerry, 29–30, 39, 123–4
Paris, 3, 52
patriotism, 103, 108, 120
Pax, Salam, 125
Peck, Rory, 133
Pentagon, 62, 73, 74
PFLP (Popular Front for the Liberation of
    Palestine), 111
Philo, Greg, 53, 81, 136
Politburo, ix
politics, 2, 8, 10, 12, 16, 18, 24, 25, 27,
    29, 49, 73–4, 79, 81, 85, 129
Politkovskaya, Anna, 7, 49, 55–7
post-traumatic stress disorder, 8
power, x, 4, 13, 16, 19–21, 49, 52, 61,
    63–4, 66–9, 87–8, 122, 132
PR (public relations), xi, 7, 66–73, 70–3,
    75–9 81–3, 89
Prague, ix, xiii
Prentoulis, Maria, 48, 54, 55, 104, 106,
    109

press, iv, 13, 18, 20–1, 40, 76, 92, 95, 98,
    123, 133
producers, 3, 4, 41, 81, 91, 93, 106, 110,
    113, 122, 127–8, 130
propaganda, xii, 7, 13–14, 20–1, 61, 66,
    82–3, 127, 129, 132
Protsyuk, Taras, 40
Prussians, 25
publication, iv, 16, 33, 126, 139
Putin, Vladimir, 32, 35, 69, 71, 102

radio, 7, 14–15, 18–19, 27, 37, 42–3, 46,
    58, 88, 90–4, 115, 128
Rafah, 90, 101
rape, 56
readers, xiii, 2, 6, 10, 37, 56–7, 121, 128
realpolitik, 80
Reed, John, 13, 22, 62–4
refugees, 41, 54, 90, 94, 114–15, 118
reporting, controlled, 32–5, 45
reporting, open, 32–5, 45
reporters, vii, ix–x, xiii, 1–5, 7, 8–13,
    15–16, 18–20, 22–5, 28–44,
    46–55, 60–4, 72, 77, 82–3, 85,
    88–91, 94–5, 98–100, 102–6,
    108–11, 113, 115–21, 124, 126,
    129–30, 132–8
research, viii, 3, 7, 43, 53, 64, 66, 83–4,
    104, 115
researchers, 3, 67, 104
resources, 7, 64, 70, 76, 83, 88, 112, 125
Reuters, 1, 4, 8, 20, 77, 87, 122, 131
revolution, 13, 62–3, 64
rifles, 11, 63
rights, iv, 46, 49, 69, 79, 80, 123
risk, 6, 28, 30, 33, 39, 41, 61, 78, 80, 89,
    98, 103, 108, 130, 133
Robinson, Piers, 9, 13, 29, 31, 37, 42, 64,
    67, 83, 84, 95, 99, 123, 129, 132
Russell, James, 9–10, 25, 27, 29, 126,
    128, 138
Russell, William Howard, 9–13, 23, 25,
    27, 28–9, 126–7, 129, 138
Russia, xiv, 7, 10, 13, 32, 44, 49, 53, 59,
    66, 68–71, 73, 75, 78–80, 83, 92
Russophobia, 75

Saakaskvili, Mikheil, 71–2, 75, 140
safety, 6, 21, 23, 31, 33, 39–41, 45, 51,
    61, 92
Saigon, 17, 77
Sambrook, Richard, 8, 138
Sarajevo, 88, 118
Sarkozy, Nicolas, 69

Schudson, Michael, 66
Scoop (novel by Evelyn Waugh), xi, 95, 123
secrecy, 40
security, 8, 33–4, 36, 39– 41, 51, 59, 62, 80, 82, 85, 87, 110, 116–17, 130, 134
Seib, Philip, 23, 85–6, 99, 106
separatists, 32, 44, 68, 69, 92
September 11th, 2, 10, 27, 47, 60, 67, 73–4, 75, 82, 106–9, 115, 119–20, 123, 139–40
shells, 16, 40, 42–3, 70
Shia, 123
Shifa (hospital, Gaza), 112, 113
Siberia, 75
Sinn Fein, 131
Sky News, 5
SNG (satellite newsgathering), 18
sniper, 39, 42
social networking, 5, 37, 85–7, 130–2, 134
soldiers, 11, 13, 23, 27, 34, 36, 41, 49, 55, 60, 63, 66, 90, 94, 102, 104, 116, 117, 126, 127, 128, 129, 133
Somerville, Stephen, 77, 131
Sontag, Susan, 16, 81, 140
Sonwalkar, Prasun, 81
sources, iv, 3, 4, 8, 20, 30, 37, 46, 61, 64, 71, 72, 78, 79, 87, 97, 113, 116, 117, 123–7, 130, 132–6, 138
Soviet Union 2, 13, 19, 38, 69, 109
'specurant' 91
spin, 49, 74–5, 83, 89, 99, 132
Sreberny, Annabelle, 89, 108
Stalin, Joseph, 72
Starye Atagi, 56
states, x, 5, 67, 69, 85, 96, 106
Stewart, Rebecca, 132
storytellers, 56
storytelling, vii, 25, 84–5, 87, 89, 91, 93, 95, 97, 99, 101, 105
strategic, 9, 25, 61, 67, 73
strategy, 12, 53, 56, 73
Streatfeild, Richard, 5, 6, 121, 126–30
Sudan, 81
suicide, xii, 44, 116
Sunni, 123
Syria, 2, 28, 87, 137
Syrian, 86–7, 131

Taliban, 5, 132, 133
Tamil Tigers, 24, 119
tanks, xiii, 12, 38, 42–3, 71

Taylor, Philip, 81
Tbilisi, 1, 19, 20, 21, 44, 68, 72, 117
technology, 4, 6, 7, 8, 10, 12, 14, 17, 18, 22, 24–8, 30, 35, 37, 45, 66, 67, 74, 75, 79, 80, 84–7, 97, 99, 101, 119, 123, 126, 129, 131–2, 134, 137, 138, 139
television, ix, xi, xiii, 1, 3, 15–21, 23, 27, 30, 31, 33, 46, 58, 59, 61, 64, 77–8, 82, 88, 91–5, 100, 105–6, 115, 118, 122, 123, 130, 133, 140
terrorists, 2, 56, 130, 132
terrorism, xii, 73, 131
terrorists, 46, 47, 96
Thatcher, Margaret, 131
Thomson, Alex, 62, 77
Thussu, Daya, 15, 17–18, 59, 88
Tikrit, 61
Times, The, 9, 10, 17, 56, 76, 124–5, 130, 137, 140
torture, 122
training, 1
translation, 32, 43, 52, 116
trauma, 59, 104, 106–7, 109, 115, 116
troops, xi, xii, 5, 11, 12, 14, 28, 29, 31–2, 34, 37, 38, 40–2, 46–7, 54, 56–7, 60, 63, 69, 71, 75, 80, 97, 109, 117, 120, 122, 130, 140
truth, xi, 48, 50–1, 57, 64, 73, 83, 86, 95, 100, 114, 117
tsar, 64, 140
Tumber, Howard, 15, 22, 29–31, 38–9, 43, 48, 54–5, 68, 80, 84, 86, 89, 94, 99, 103, 106, 109, 117, 123–4, 140
Tunisia, 2
Twitter, 86–8, 138, 139
tyranny, ix, 122

UEFA, 92
UGC (user-generated content), 4, 8, 23, 86, 97–9, 101, 137
Umm Qasr, xi
Union of Soviet Socialist Republics, 69 (see also Soviet Union)
United Kingdom, iv, 100, 118, 122, 129
United Nations, 18, 40, 88, 89, 103, 105
United States, iv, xii, xiii, 2, 5, 15–17, 21–3, 32, 35, 37, 40, 47, 51, 60–1, 62, 67, 69, 71, 73–4, 77, 80–1, 100, 106–9, 117, 120–5, 132, 136, 138

universities, viii, 3, 8, 53
uprisings, 86–7, 135, 137, 139
USB cable, 129
Utiashvili, Shota, 68, 71

values, xiii, 24, 74, 79, 81, 83, 132
veterans, x, 53, 118
video, 4, 5, 25, 59, 86
videotapes, 77
Vietnam, xii, 6, 15–17, 19, 27, 29, 33,
    66–7, 77, 84, 100, 102, 117, 131
violence, 58–9, 65, 96, 108, 119, 133
Vladikavkaz, 92

Waisbord, Silvio, 47, 60, 108
war, viii, x, xii, xiii, 1, 2, 3, 4, 6, 8, 9, 10,
    12, 14–20, 27, 29, 35, 38, 39, 45,
    52, 53, 55, 59, 60, 62, 66, 68, 74,
    75, 77, 79, 80, 81, 83, 84, 103,
    104, 111, 115, 117, 118, 123, 131,
    132, 138, 139, 140
warfare, 62, 73, 74, 78, 103, 130
WarLogs (Wikileaks), 133
warriors, 1, 2, 5, 77, 78, 79, 134, 138

Washington, 6, 87, 106, 108, 115
Waterloo, Battle of, 9, 25–6, 126
weapons, 54, 58, 63, 66, 67, 77, 100,
    116, 117, 122, 123
websites, 5, 46, 87, 90, 91, 93, 97, 98,
    104, 111, 130, 138, 140
Webster, Frank, 22, 29, 30, 31, 38, 80,
    84, 86, 89, 94, 99, 103, 140
Wenceslas Square, ix, x
Wikileaks, 133
Wright, Evan, 35–7, 41, 45
writing, viii, 2, 3, 5, 6, 16, 27, 36, 39, 48,
    62, 67, 69, 77, 86, 87, 88, 99,
    107, 119, 125, 126, 128, 137,
    139

Yeltsin, Boris, xiv, 80
Yemen, 2
Yerevan, 1
ynet, 130
Yugloslavia, 18, 19, 53

Zelizer, Barbie, 29, 30, 31, 37, 106, 107,
    109